TWAYNE'S WORLD AUTHORS SERIES

A Survey of the World's Literature

GERMANY

Ulrich Weisstein, Indiana University

EDITOR

Novalis

TWAS 556

NOVALIS

FRIEDR. v. HARDENBERG.
GEB. D. 2. MAI 1772
GEST. D. 25. MAERZ 1801.

Novalis

NOVALIS

By JOHN NEUBAUER

University of Pittsburgh

TWAYNE PUBLISHERS

A DIVISION OF G. K. HALL & CO., BOSTON

Library of Congress Cataloging in Publication Data

Neubauer, John, 1933–
Novalis.

(Twayne's world authors series ; TWAS 556 : Germany)
Bibliography: p. 176– 80
Includes index.
1. Hardenberg, Friedrich, Freiherr von,
1772–1801—Criticism and interpretation.
PT2291.Z5N44   831'.6   79-14958
ISBN 0-8057-6398-8

Contents

About the Author

John Neubauer studied at Amherst College and received his advanced degrees, an M.S. in physics and a Ph.D. in German, from Northwestern University. He has held teaching appointments at Princeton University, Case Western Reserve University, and the University of Pittsburgh. At the University of Pittsburgh he was Chairman of the Department of Germanic Languages from 1973 to 1978, and is currently professor of German with Secondary Appointment in History and Philosophy of Science. In addition, he has been a visiting professor at the Universidad del Valle, Cali, Colombia, the University of British Columbia, and Harvard University. He received a Fulbright Research Grant for 1972–73.

Professor Neubauer's publications include *Bifocal Vision. Novalis' Philosophy of Nature and Disease, Symbolismus und symbolische Logik. Die Idee der Ars Combinatoria in der Entwicklung der modernen Dichtung*, and articles in *Deutsche Vierteljahrsschrift, Neophilologus, Sudhoffs Archiv, Journal of the History of Ideas, German Quarterly, German Life and Letters*, and *Yearbook of Comparative and General Literature*.

Preface

When, in the late 1960s, radical German demonstrators were chanting that Novalis' "blue flower," symbol of German Romanticism, be colored red, a doctoral student set out to show that the slogan was senseless, for Novalis' flower had always been red: by demanding that the imagination reign supreme and that the present be annihilated, Novalis was a visionary kin of Walter Benjamin, Ernst Bloch, and Herbert Marcuse.[1]

The incident testifies to Novalis' continued presence, but it also demonstrates that disagreements about him are generated by image and ideology rather than by the substance of his writings. The blue flower has wafted through German classrooms and living rooms for many generations, and Novalis has become synonymous with the problematic political legacy of German Romanticism. As a conservative critic recently remarked, the blue flower "has been the target of yearning for our fathers and grandfathers, who wanted to get out of the self-created machine world, the world of the masses, means, and mechanisms, into an envisioned realm of freedom and harmony."[2] Since a similar view, with negative connotation, is held by East German critics and historians, Novalis has not been accepted into the canonized heritage of the German Democratic Republic.[3]

English-speaking readers have luckily been spared an ideologized Novalis, but they have been deprived also of a major poet and a key figure of European Romanticism. The few English translations of his works do not convey the power of the original, and excepting Carlyle's essay from 1829, few critics have tried to introduce him to a larger reading public. The present volume cannot make up for all this neglect but may prove to be a small step toward it. Within the guidelines of this series, I have attempted to offer English-speaking readers a general introduction to Novalis, giving, wherever possible, samples of his writings. I have tried to strike a balance between descriptive accounts, summaries of scholarship, and original contributions. The organization has been dictated by the unique nature of Novalis' genius. Since he applied his imagination not only to the arts, but also to philosophy, science, and his own life, always seeking to integrate these different realms, the usual division into "life" and "work" did not seem to be appropriate. The short biographical chapter covers, therefore, only his early years. In the remaining chapters, I have tried to show the interrelation between his life and his writings and to offer a corrective to earlier views, which often conceived of Novalis' "poetization of life" in a naive fashion. The breadth and complexity of Novalis' genius can be best appreciated if the flights of his imagination are seen side by side with the sobriety and seriousness he showed in studying, working, and tackling everyday problems.

In attempting to provide a fresh view of Novalis, I have gratefully relied on the new historical-critical edition of his works, which does indeed throw a new light on the logic and consistency of his mind. The references given in the body of my text will be to the volumes and pages of that edition: I have occasionally modernized the spelling in the German quotations to ease the task of English-speaking readers. To Professor Richard Samuel, chief editor of the *Schriften,* I owe an extraordinary debt. Ever since I became interested in Novalis, he has helped and advised me with that kindness that is unique to him. This book would be superior had it materialized as the joint project which we originally planned it to be. Since the present version developed in consultations with him, he should share the credit for its virtues. For its shortcomings I am fully responsible.

I am indebted to my colleague Dee Ashliman for reading some of the chapters and suggesting improvements. Professor Ulrich Weisstein's sharp eye quickly spotted my faulty passages, and I am deeply grateful to him for the prompt and thorough reading he gave to the manuscript.

JOHN NEUBAUER

University of Pittsburgh

Chronology

1772 May 2: Friedrich von Hardenberg born on the family estate, Oberwiederstedt, in Thuringia.

1784 Novalis' father appointed director of the Saxon salt mines. The family moves to the town of Weißenfels.

1789 May: Novalis meets Gottfried August Bürger, author of *Lenore*.

1790 June to October: studies at the *Gymnasium* of Eisleben, where the classical philologist Christian David Jani is headmaster. October–September 1791: attends the University of Jena. Meets frequently with Friedrich Schiller and the Kantian philosopher Karl Leonhard Reinhold.

1791 April: Wieland publishes Novalis' poem "Klagen eines Jünglings" in *Der Neue Deutsche Merkur*. October–March 1793: attends the University of Leipzig. Friendship with Friedrich Schlegel.

1792 December-March 1793: love affair with Julie Eisenstück.

1793 May 27: matriculation at the University of Wittenberg.

1794 June 14: graduates in law from Wittenberg. October: begins administrative training in Tennstedt with the *Kreisamtsmann* (district director) Coelestin August Just. November 17: meets the twelve and one-half year old Sophie von Kühn during an official visit at the estate of Grüningen.

1795 March 15: secret engagement to Sophie. May: meets Fichte and Hölderlin. The serious study of Fichte's philosophy starts in the fall. November 9: Sophie falls ill.

1796 January: studies chemistry under Johann Christian Wiegleb. February: assumes the post of assistant administrator of the Saxon salt mines under his father.

1797 March 19: death of Sophie von Kühn. April 14: death of Novalis' brother Erasmus. April 18–July 6: keeps a diary entitled "Mourning." May 13: mystic experience at Sophie's grave. August: visits August Wilhelm and Caroline Schlegel in Jena. Fall: studies Kant, Hemsterhuis, and Fichte. December: meets Schelling on his way to Freiberg, where he embarks upon scientific and technical studies, chiefly under the geologist Abraham Gottlob Werner.

1798   January: meets Julie von Charpentier. March 29: meets Goethe. May: publication of *Blütenstaub* (Pollen) in *Athenäum;* begins the writing of *Die Lehrlinge zu Sais (The Novices at Sais).* June-July: Publication of *Glauben und Liebe (Faith and Love)* in *Jahrbücher der Preußischen Monarchie.* July 15–mid-August: cure in Teplitz, Bohemia. August 25–26: meeting of the Romantics, visit of the Dresden Gallery. September: starts entries for the "Allgemeines Brouillon," an encyclopedia project. December: engagement to Julie von Charpentier.

1799   May: return to Weißenfels. May 20: participates with von Oppel in an inspection tour of the Saxon salt works. July 17: beginning of the friendship with Ludwig Tieck. Fall: writes most of the *Geistliche Lieder (Devotional Songs)* and the speech *Die Christenheit oder Europa (Christendom or Europe).* November 11–14: meeting of the Romantics in August Wilhelm Schlegel's house in Jena. Novalis reads his *Geistliche Lieder* and *Christenheit.* December 7: appointment as assessor and member of the directorate of the Saxon salt mines. December-January 1800: finishes the *Hymnen an die Nacht (Hymns to the Night).*

1800   January-April: writes the first part of *Heinrich von Ofterdingen.* April 10: applies for the position of *Amtshauptmann* (circuit director). June 1–16: leads a geological survey as part of a comprehensive study of Saxony carried out under Werner. August: publication of the *Hymnen an die Nacht* in *Athenäum.* September or October: outbreak of fatal illness. October 13: journey to Dresden for medical treatment. December 6: appointment as circuit director.

1801   January 21: brought back from Dresden to Weißenfels in very poor health. March 25: dies in Weißenfels in the presence of Friedrich Schlegel.

CHAPTER 1

Preparation

I *Childhood and University Studies*

GEORG Friedrich Philipp von Hardenberg, who entered literary history under the pen name of Novalis, was born on May 2, 1772, at Oberwiederstedt, an estate some forty kilometers northwest of Halle, acquired by a branch of his ancient family in the seventeenth century. His father, Baron Heinrich Ulrich Erasmus von Hardenberg, had a turbulent youth, but later converted to Count Zinzendorf's Moravian Brethren, a sect usually referred to as "Herrnhuter," after their colony in the area of Oberlausitz, Saxony. Novalis was the second child and first-born son of Erasmus von Hardenberg's second marriage to Auguste Bernhardine von Boelzig.

According to his brother Carl, Novalis fell seriously ill at the age of nine but developed rapidly afterwards.[1] One of his first private tutors, C. Chr. E. Schmid, became a professor of philosophy in Jena and remembered Novalis as a "susceptible, independent, original, and imaginative boy" (IV, 568). The strict and frugal household of the Hardenbergs was governed by the "Herrnhuter" rules, but the father was frequently on the road, and the education of the children was largely left to the pliant and loving mother.

In 1784, the father was appointed director of the Saxon salt mines, and the family moved to the medium-sized town of Weißenfels, about thirty kilometers southwest of Leipzig. Their financial situation improved somewhat thereby, and they were able to move into a large four story house that still exists. Soon afterwards, Novalis was sent to his paternal uncle in Lucklum, where he stayed for a year. Friedrich Wilhelm Hardenberg, a high master of the Teutonic Order and a socially distinguished and powerful man, treated his

11

brother and his family with condescension, and Novalis later on had difficulty in asserting himself against his domineering help and conservative views. One of the outstanding events in Novalis' life during these years was his meeting with the poet Gottfried August Bürger, author of the famous ballad "Lenore"; it kindled his poetic ambitions and resulted in a torrent of poetic works and projects, most of them ornate and imitative, not testifying to any great poetic talent.

In 1790, after years of private tutoring, Novalis was sent to the *Gymnasium* of Eisleben, whose headmaster, Christian David Jani, was a highly respected classical scholar. However, Jani died barely four months after Novalis' arrival, and since Novalis was found advanced enough to enter the university, he matriculated in Jena in October 1790. He had a good grounding in the classics and, as his inventory of books taken to Jena shows, was widely read.

Novalis participated in the loud and boisterous student life of Jena, including the duels, but he received his lasting impressions from the Kantian philosopher Reinhold and from Friedrich Schiller, who was at that time professor of history there. He had close personal contact with Schiller and probably attended his lectures on the history of European nations and the crusades. But Schiller's main influence was surely to reinforce Novalis' poetic inclinations and to lead him away from the study of law. This caused such a concern to Novalis' father that he appealed to Schiller to convince his son that, as a first-born, he had to prepare himself for an administrative career and become a supporter of the family (IV, 570). As a result, Novalis transferred to the University of Leipzig in October 1791, writing letters full of youthful enthusiasm and adulation to Schiller, and acknowledging that a single word from Schiller had a greater effect on him than repeated warnings and lessons by others (IV, 90). He read *Don Carlos* and dedicated himself to the Schillerian ideals of beauty, moral grace, and friendship. His admiration for the older poet continued even after his best friend, Friedrich Schlegel, had serious clashes with Schiller.

That Novalis did not follow his pledges and continued to lead a carefree life in Leipzig was mainly due to his newly found friendship with Schlegel. Friedrich Schlegel was of Novalis' age, but more experienced in worldly matters; he came to Leipzig from the University of Göttingen, ostensibly to study law, but plunging into everything that came his way, from the classics to the natural sciences and languages. He was a brilliant, unbalanced, but imposing young man, who treated Novalis with some condescension because he thought "fate had played into his hands" (IV, 571) a "very cheerful, very soft" young man who "assumed every shape impressed upon him" (IV, 572). Nevertheless, Novalis' "serenity of youth," his "chastity which had its foundation in the so l and not in inexperience" (IV, 572), greatly impressed Schlegel. The friends had different temperaments, and their relation was not always harmonious, but their friendship proved to be resilient and deep in the long run. The conversations, the correspondence, the exchange of notebooks, and the "symphilosophy" with Schlegel gave, without any doubt, the most important intellectual and artistic impetus to Novalis. As for Schlegel, he closed his fragment collection *Ideen* in the *Athenäum* (1800) with a message "To Novalis:" "You do not hover at the fringe, for it is in your spirit that poetry and philosophy have interpenetrated intimately. Your spirit stood closest to me in these images of uncomprehended truth. I think what you have thought; what I thought, you will think or have thought already. There are misunderstandings that reconfirm the highest accordance" (III, 493). Novalis replied by jotting on the margin of the manuscript: "The thought that you are my friend and that you have addressed to me these deeply felt words engenders a magnificent feeling in me. I know that we agree in many things and believe that we are truly at one because the same hope and desire constitute our life and death" (III, 493).

Friedrich and his older brother August Wilhelm became the center of the early German Romantics, primarily through the publication of their journal *Athenäum* (1798–1800) and through the hospitable home that August Wilhelm kept after he moved to Jena in 1796. In addition to Novalis and the Schlegel brothers, the circle included August Wilhelm's attractive wife Caroline, who later married another member of the circle, the philosopher Friedrich Wilhelm Schelling. Ludwig Tieck became a personal friend of Novalis in 1799; two other members, the theologian Friedrich Schleiermacher and Friedrich Schlegel's wife Dorothea, née Mendelssohn, came in contact with the group during Friedrich's stay in Berlin. The somewhat older philosopher, Johann Gottlob Fichte, exercised an enormous intellectual and personal power over all of them. With the death of Novalis in 1801, the group fell apart.

Novalis' younger brother, Erasmus, joined him in Leipzig in 1792, and for a while, as Novalis recalled later, the two played "brilliant roles on the stage of the world" (IV, 127). Erasmus, who died only five years later, had a special affection for his older brother and was probably closest to Novalis in the whole family. By the end of the year, Novalis had fallen in love with the daughter of a textile manufacturer, and contemplating marriage, he approached his uncle for aid to start a career in the army. Both the uncle and the father were upset by the prospect of a middle class marriage and refused help; the affair ended ignominiously, and Novalis left Leipzig to enroll at the University of Wittenberg. This time he kept his social life under control and managed to obtain his law degree on June 14, 1794, in two semesters.

II Engagement

Between June and October 1794, Novalis stayed with his family in Weißenfels, playing billiards, drinking, dancing, and courting girls with his brother Carl. A record of these happy days is his poem on the waltz (I, 385), a dance at that time still regarded as vulgar by the establishment.

When it became evident that neither the uncle nor the Prussian minister Karl August von Hardenberg, a distant relative and key figure in the later Prussian reforms, could quickly secure a position in the Prussian civil service for Novalis, father Hardenberg decided to make his son an apprentice to Coelestin August Just, the highly respected district director of Thuringia. Just, at that time a bachelor living in Tennstedt, welcomed the young man, who was conscientious and yet much more than a bureaucrat. Novalis' lifelong attachment to Just extended also to his niece, Caroline, and later to Just's wife, Rachel. Just recalls in his biography of Novalis: "I was supposed to become his teacher and leader, but he was my teacher" (IV, 539); Novalis, in turn, felt later "the infinite usefulness" of his apprenticeship (IV, 169). Just became his friend, taught him how to be a man of business, and made Thuringia the school of his "business life" (IV, 187).

Visits with the landowners of the district provided a welcome relief to the otherwise dull job. During one such visit, on November 17, 1794, Novalis came to know the family of Captain Johann Rudolf von Rockenthien in the neighboring Grüningen, and fell head over heels in love with the captain's stepdaughter, Sophie von Kühn, then less than thirteen years old. Fearing that his father would not consent to a marriage with a girl of small means, Novalis kept the engagement secret until June of that year but in the end his father was completely taken by the bride. Novalis' brothers came to regard Grüningen as paradise and dreamed of marriages with Sophie's sisters.

When hopes for a job in Prussia dimmed, the father requested a position in his directorate for Novalis, which was granted in December 1795. Novalis was eager to embark on a career to support a family, prepared himself with a two week course in chemistry, and moved back home to assume the job in February 1796. But the father's "blind religious fanaticism," his "violent dislike for everything called innovation" (IV, 371), as well as other domestic problems must have made his life difficult, for Novalis' letters from this period are replete with complaints. His troubles were compounded when on November 9, 1795, Sophie fell seriously ill, apparently with a tumor of the liver. She seemed to be recuperating well during the following winter and spring, but in July 1796 she had to be operated on by Johann Christian Stark, Schiller's physician in Jena. In spite of two additional surgical attempts to clean the infected wound, she entered a long agony which terminated with her death on March 19, 1797. Novalis had departed from her a few days earlier, unable to witness her suffering; barely four weeks later he was similarly driven from home because of the imminent consumptive death of his brother Erasmus. Within a month he lost the two people who were perhaps closest to him.

We shall want to uncover the actual psychological motives from underneath the accumulated legend, without casting doubt on the sincerity of Novalis' love for Sophie. By all accounts, Sophie was a charming child, and Novalis took pleasure at the spontaneity and playful earthiness of the Rockenthiens, so different from the somber pietism of his own home. But Sophie was actually of Lolita age, and the naive tone and faulty spelling of her few extant writings suggest that she was intellectually as unequal a partner as she was sexually.[2] Erasmus warned Novalis that he would have to give up that "brilliant role" he played on the world stage (IV, 369), and that he would probably reconsider his decision during the years of waiting (IV, 366).

The object of Novalis' infatuation was surely more the product of his imagination than Sophie's mind and body. Attempting to suppress his powerful sexual urges, he fought against fantasy and daydreaming because he believed that sickly imagination engendered "sickly sensibility and sickly intellect" (IV, 117). One day before meeting Sophie, he confessed to a friend "that a true pandemonium seemed to exist in the old smoky office, where the devil of lust was continuously vexing him, dancing with voluptuous images on the paper in front of him" (IV, 147). For guidance and calming influence, he often sought the company of women who were sexually unattainable for him. He wrote to Caroline Just immediately after having met Sophie that Caroline's company would perhaps provide him with the means to grind off the excesses of his excitable imagination (IV, 149), while of Sophie's sister he asked later: "Be my educator, my counsellor, my friend [. . .] peace, intelligent sense, taste, and uplifting—this is what I hope to learn in your school [. . .] I will perhaps be unhappy, for nature made me excitable" (IV, 166).

But if he feared the sexual fantasies of loneliness, he was equally wary of the physical act itself. He was sexually experienced, but reporting about his first encounter with Sophie, he confessed to Erasmus that his "tender feelings" were usually destroyed once he received "vulgar signs of favor." Between the extremes of pure sexual fantasy and illusionless sex, the relationship to Sophie must have seemed a satisfactory compromise, for she was a real and as yet unavailable object of desire: Sophie was the promise of Novalis' future sexual and domestic bliss. The latter he envisioned in a playful sketch sent to Caroline Just (IV, 151); the sexual fantasies about Sophie surfaced only after her death, when he recast his future-oriented love as a reunion after death: "In death is love the sweetest; for a lover death is a wedding night" (IV, 50). The unique fusion of eroticism and death wish in some of Novalis' best lyric poetry feeds on precisely that original anticipatory sexual fantasy which after her death became a yearning to reunite in the future realm.

Thus Novalis' lifelong attachment to Sophie retained its essential character amidst metamorphoses. While some of the original passion gave way to a reflection which drew universal conclusions from the personal fate, reflection was already present in the fateful first meeting, if one is to judge by Erasmus' response to Novalis' account of it. While his brother responded with the usual cautionary advice not to be blinded by sudden fits of passion, he also commented that he did not like the tragic tone and "the cold, determined spirit that dominated the whole letter" (IV, 368). Novalis apparently replied that he needed steadiness and persistence of character to concentrate on a single task, and marriage was the means to achieve this (IV, 370)—a remarkably sober explanation which puts passion into the service of self-improvement. This may have been a mere ploy to demonstrate sobriety, but the very use of the cunning argument would negate the supposition that he was seized by "blind passion." In fact, he never painted Sophie and Grüningen with more attractive colors than they possessed, and this helped him later to weather the quarrels with Sophie or confrontations with what he called the "seamier side" of Grüningen (IV, 159).

The most remarkable document of his clear perception is perhaps the short character sketch of Sophie entitled "Klarisse" (IV, 24f.), written during the summer of 1796. She is described there as obedient to her father and respectful of others, sensitive, averse to small talk, charitable, and "more complete, more free than we are, for she doesn't want to be anything, she is." She smoked and loved wine, but feared ghosts, spiders, and mice, and did not believe in an afterlife. While Novalis may have regarded some of these features as charming idiosyncrasies, he was surely concerned that she had no interest in poetry, that she was dominating and frightened by the idea of marriage and that she expected him to be constantly in good humor. His love was often burdensome to her, and she was "generally cold." In the long run, these attitudes would surely have created friction; but she fell ill, compassion overshadowed everything, and he came to love her "almost more because of her sickness" (IV, 190). Thus clarity of perception and a loving refashioning of the perceptions went hand in hand. The hallmark of Novalis' mature wisdom was to comprehend lucidly the cold recalcitrant facts and yet to adapt them to his emotional needs, to endow them with an aura of his imagination. He did this quite consciously, not, as is commonly thought, to escape from the oppressive facts of life, but to integrate them into his personal growth.[3]

III *Mourning and Awakening*

In the weeks following Sophie's death, Novalis occasionally conveyed his grief to others in poetic and melodramatic images: "Evening came to surround me while I continued to look into the dawn. My mourning is as boundless as my love" (IV, 206); "The desperate player throws down the cards and smiles, as if awakened from a

dream by the nightwatchman's last call; he awaits the dawn which
cheers him to a fresh life in the real world" (IV, 218). However,
the diary that Novalis kept between April 18 and July 6, 1797,
dating the entries from the day of Sophie's death, is different. While
it, too, registers moments of loneliness or terrified memories of
Sophie's suffering, it may not be regarded as spontaneous expression
and precipitation of grief, for its dominant theme is the struggle to
endow the senseless deaths of his fiancée and his brother with a
"higher" meaning. Its dominant mode is reflection and self-obser-
vation in search of clarity and control. The brute and unalterable
fact of death must be used to ignite the imagination, and this
imagination must be domesticated, be put in the service of an intense spirituality.

To begin with, the diary is an astonishingly frank record of "sensuous fantasies," of lust, yearning, and once even of a resultant
"explosion." The struggle against this life-asserting power is par-
alleled by steadfast attempts to adhere to an "engagement in higher
sense" (IV, 211)—namely, to join Sophie in death. Novalis did not
plan to commit suicide, but strove rather for a state of sobriety,
moderation, and serenity (IV, 48) in which he could "wait for the
moment that will call me" (IV, 46). He wanted to die "happily like
a young poet" (IV, 45), to fulfill his "calling to an invisible world"
(IV, 213), and to demonstrate the possibility of a "higher love" (IV,
38). He regarded his sorrow as a quiet flame which would consume
him, enabling him to rise from the ashes to a new life (IV, 209 and
218)—a phoenix motif which was to become central to the *Hymnen
an die Nacht* (*Hymns to the Night*).

Though "future existence was nascent" in him (IV, 221), almost
daily entries indicate that the adherence to the pledge was not easy.
Worry that his death would bring new grief to his family and friends
(IV, 36 and 43) was less of an obstacle than was his own dogged
love of life. Since he had been too strongly attached to happiness
in this world (IV, 213f.), he sought to divert his attention from trivial
pleasantries, such as Friedrich Schlegel's gossipy, witty, polemical,
and flamboyant company, which he found "ruinous" (IV, 48f.).
(Schlegel, in turn, was aggravated by what he mistakenly characterized as excessive *Herrenhuter* pietism.) Novalis wanted to relate
everything to the idea of Sophie (IV, 37), to establish her image as
the pivotal point around which his whole life would revolve. But
he frequently fell short of that intensification of memory and antic-

ipation which would have enabled him to behold her image: "Now I seem to be [. . .] cold and too much in the mood of everyday life. [. . .] Strive only for the higher, permanent reflection and its mood. Oh! that I am so incapable of remaining elevated" (IV, 33). No wonder! His union with his beloved required a constant exercise of that imagination which supplied him with the lurid images of his sexual desires as well; the fusion of eroticism with his search for a "higher life" succeeded only in his later poetry.

The self-conscious strengthening of the imagination throughout these months is the background of the famous experience at Sophie's grave on May 13 which provided the point of departure for the *Hymnen an die Nacht:* "I was indescribably happy there—moments of flashing enthusiasm—I blew the grave away like dust—centuries were like moments—her presence was palpable—I believed she would step forward any minute" (IV, 35 f.). The key passage from the third hymn poetically reformulates the experience:

Zur Staubwolke wurde der Hügel—durch die Wolke sah ich die verklärten Züge der Geliebten. In Ihren Augen ruhte die Ewigkeit [. . .] Jahrtausende zogen abwärts in die Ferne, wie Ungewitter. (I, 135)

(The mound became a cloud of dust—through the cloud I saw the transfigured features of the beloved. Eternity rested in her eyes [. . .] Millenia moved off into the distance like storms.)

It is impossible to say whether Novalis actually "saw" Sophie or was merely seized by the certainty of her presence, as some interpreters believe.[4] But there is considerable evidence that the "vision" was the fruit of deliberate efforts, which included stimulation through the contemplation of her grave, her letters, and other mementos, and the reading of appropriate literary and philosophical texts. From the outset, Novalis employed spiritual exercises to intensely remember Sophie and to conjure up her image. Eight days before the "vision" he recorded in his diary: "I held quite sharply an image of 'Söffchen' before me—in profile, next to me on the sofa—in the green scarf—in characteristic situations, in dresses, does she appear to me most readily. In the evening I thought of her generally quite ardently" (IV, 33). On March 28, he wrote to Caroline Just that his hope for a continued bond with Sophie would be strengthened "if Sophie could and would be allowed to appear to me. How unspeakably happy would I be already here on earth if she would reveal herself occasionally to me, would uplift and strengthen me if only with a single loving glance. How transfigured would I live in myself. I do not yet give up this hope" (IV, 211).

In order to become receptive to such a vision, he frequently visited the grave and engaged there in contemplation. He also focused his mind and imagination by reading: his preoccupation with Goethe's *Wilhelm Meisters Lehrjahre (Wilhelm Meister's Apprenticeship)* perhaps in preparation of a critical review, and a cursory reading of Young's "Night Thoughts" were followed by a reading of August Wilhelm Schlegel's translation of *Romeo and Juliet* just hours before his "vision" (IV, 35). Retrospectively, Novalis thought that Shakespeare's greatness lay in his ability to engender "divinatory dispositions" (IV, 227). The crucial reading experience was a letter that his brother Carl wrote two days before the "vision," telling how a storm outside engendered in him a wish to die: "I could think with genuine serenity of the sudden death by lightning [. . .] a moment, and one would be—*there*, dear good Fritz, in the eternal embrace of our beloved ones" (IV, 483).

Carl's subsequent discussion of death relies heavily on a passage in Jean Paul's novel *Die unsichtbare Loge (The Invisible Lodge),* leading to the conclusion that there are rare moments when one may easily pierce through "the haze of the few years that force themselves between us and the grave, when these years appear short as if one had lived through them already; if we could acquire the habit of such bright, easy insights we would probably live happier" (IV, 484). Carl's reflections on his physical and literary experiences imposed themselves on Novalis' mind and affected his "vision" at the grave, or at least the accounts of it, which are full of verbal reminiscences. His diary account and his third hymn describe a state of ecstasy where time seems suspended, the soul rises from its earthly prison, and the eye shifts from the grave to pierce the clouds and penetrate into an invisible world. Since Carl suggested that graves are cheerful and friendly invitations to join friends, Novalis may have felt a renewed urge to search for an ecstatic moment through contemplation at the grave: he "worked" toward a mystic experience, and his "vision" resulted from exercises aimed at acquiring the ability to generate "definite moods" "at will" (IV, 40).

Awareness of such deliberate efforts should not detract from an appreciation of Novalis' "vision," for great mystic experiences are often the result of severe spiritual exercises. The documents in Novalis' case merely indicate that his experience, whatever its nature, did not come from an abandonment of the self to an external possessive force but rather through an activation of the imagination. The activation of the imagination (rather than of the emotions) endowed the period of mourning with special significance in Novalis' poetic development. "Life in Sophie" demanded a creative transformation of reality, as well as a redefinition of her as guardian and redeemer. The reshaping of Sophie's image is observable already in the diary's new calendar: by choosing the date of her death as a point of departure, Novalis designated her, perhaps unconsciously, as his personal savior. In subsequent weeks she became the "transfigured" (IV, 211) and the "chosen" one (IV, 41), anticipating the merger with the "mediator" figure of Christ which took place later in the hymns and songs. Indeed, the question posed on June 15—"without her, what do I have?"—was later rephrased to open the *Geistliche Lieder*, referring by then to the Redeemer rather than to Sophie.

CHAPTER 2

Apprenticeship in Philosophy: 1794–1797

IN the two-and-one-half years between graduation and the resumption of his studies in Freiberg, Novalis wrote only about a dozen poems, but he made many philosophical notes, which were to provide him with rich material for years to come, even though they did not add up to a system. Several of these notebooks disappeared, but the surviving voluminous writings, only recently made available fully and in a reliable chronological order, indicate their scope and their depth. About five hundred manuscript pages, started in the fall of 1795 and finished about a year later, record Novalis' struggle with Fichte's philosophy (II, 104–296); the rest dates from 1797 and contains further studies on Fichte (II, 345–59), as well as on Kant, Hemsterhuis, and Eschenmayer (II, 360–94). Studies of Schelling and Hülsen are documented only in diaries and letters. These studies led, in 1798, to Novalis' first major publication, the fragment collection *Blütenstaub (Pollen)*.

I Fichte Studies: 1795–1796

In May 1795, Novalis spent an evening in Jena with Johann Gottlieb Fichte and the poet Friedrich Hölderlin at the house of Friedrich Immanuel Niethammer, publisher of the influential *Philosophisches Journal*. Niethammer noted in his diary that they talked much about religion and revelation and concluded that philosophy faced many unanswered questions (IV, 588). The meeting may have given Novalis the impetus to explore the problems of philosophy through a study of Fichte, a newly appointed professor of philosophy at Jena who had just published the text of his lectures *Bestimmung des Gelehrten (The Vocation of the Scholar)* and two major formulations of his "Science of Knowledge" (*Wissenschafts-*

lehre).[1] In the fall, Novalis devoted about three hours daily to "urgent introductory studies" to prepare himself for life, to fill the gaps in his knowledge, and to train his "intellectual powers" (IV, 159). Apparently he planned to publish something related to these studies, but nothing has survived (IV, 180f).

A short discussion of Fichte's abstract ideas is needed here to explain their hold on the Romantic generation and their power to force Novalis to undertake a "laborious investigation of Fichtean philosophy" (IV, 311). Like all German philosophers of his generation, Fichte formulated his ideas in response to Kant's transcendentalism, which established a careful balance between subject and object, consciousness and world. Kant's "Copernican Revolution" consisted in the proposal that the mind possessed, prior to experience, some "pure forms" (space, time, and the categories of reason) which played an active and constructive role in knowledge; but Kant limited the sphere of knowledge so constructed to the phenomenal world, and he declared the noumenal world—things in themselves—to be eternally off limits for the human mind. Asserting that the noumenal world was spiritual, Fichte and the other idealists ignored Kant's injunction. For Fichte, there were ultimately only two types of philosophers: the idealists posited an "intelligence in itself," the dogmatists (Fichte's term for materialists and determinists) a "thing in itself" as the substratum of existence. Science or logic were of no help in deciding whether to sacrifice the independence of the ego to that of the thing or vice versa.[2] "What kind of philosophy one chooses is dependent on the kind of man one is"[3]: dogmatists think that they are dependent on the forces of the material world, while idealists believe in their inner power and independence. Thus Fichte's idealism reflected his fervent belief in man's self-reliance, and his impact on his contemporaries is explainable by his ability to spread the gospel of freedom at a time when the French Revolution seemed to fail in its realization. According to Fichte, man's final and never quite realizable goal was to subjugate and control by human law everything lacking intelligence.[4]

In support of this personal belief, Fichte erected an abstract construction where everything could be deduced from the idealist premise. In place of a "thing in itself," he posited a consciousness which was no Cartesian substance but merely activity. Just as the ceaselessly striving Faust of Goethe proposes that the opening of the Gospel of Saint John should read "In the beginning was the Act," so Fichte set his idealist history in motion with a "pure act" (Tathandlung).

According to Fichte's first principle, this transcendental act of consciousness, later called "intellectual intuition," bends back upon itself,[5] so that "the ego simply posits originally its own being."[6] This ego is not the empirical self of individual minds but rather a transcendental consciousness without accidental individual properties.[7] While Fichte did not originally attribute concrete existence to his transcendental consciousness, he later saw it as a mystic God who created the material world in an emanation or overflow. The self-definition of the intellectual intuition necessitates the positing of a not-self, and thus, the boundless freedom of the self becomes limited. These two aspects of the intellectual intuition are captured in the second and third principle of Fichte's theory: "a non-ego is simply opposed to the ego," and "I posit in the ego a divisible non-ego opposed to a divisible ego."[8] This way Fichte "derives" the multiplicity of the object world (non-ego=nature) and the multiplicity of subjects (divisible, limited ego=individual consciousness). A key feature in Fichte's explanation of this process is that the positing of the non-ego is an act of the "productive imagination" (produktive Einbildungskraft) which operates on a level not immediately available to consciousness. The material world is a product of the ego, but it appears in common sense experience as something given; this enjoins us to bring into consciousness our transcendental creativity and to "recapture," as it were, the boundless freedom of the pure ego. Hence Fichte's reformulation of Kant's categorical imperative: everything should be posited in the ego; the ego should be independent and everything dependent on it. The absolute ego, because of its absoluteness, demands the conformity of the objects to the ego.[9] The task of man, especially of philosophic reflection, is to overcome the particularity of the empirical ego by slowly regaining the freedom of the pure self. In that sense, as Novalis aptly remarked, the true philosophic act is self-extinction (II, 395), or inversely, death is a genuine philosophic act (II, 374). Written during the months when he intensely wished to follow Sophie in her death, these remarks indicate how Novalis' existential and philosophic concerns coincided.

It has been widely held that early German Romanticism represented essentially a "poetically exaggerated Fichte,"[10] because the poets misappropriated the productive imagination of Fichte's pure self for the poet's whimsical self—a confusion roughly comparable to a mistaken identification of Coleridge's "primary imagination" of the finite mind with that "eternal act of creation in the infinite I AM" of which it is a repetition.[11] While the German Romantics may be accused of overestimating man's creative powers, Novalis surely did not "misread" Fichte, for, in part, this is where he disagreed with his mentor. He knew well that the empirical subject, being "simultaneously the whole and the part" (II, 134), had to become alienated and abstracted from itself (II, 137 and 150) in order to turn into a pure self.

Novalis' disagreements with Fichte are evident in the very style of his notes. Concentrating on the abstract and deductive arguments in the theoretical part of the *Wissenschaftslehre*, he writes a more relaxed prose that often resorts to dialogues, reconsiderations of earlier points, asides, and reflections. His gradual dissatisfaction with abstract philosophizing culminates in a demand for a new kind of philosophy: "The true philosophic system must be freedom and infinitude, or, to express it pointedly, lack of system brought under a system. Only such a system can avoid the mistakes of a system and not be accused either of injustice or of anarchy" (II, 289). The remark foreshadows Novalis' later practice of writing fragmentary and aphoristic utterances and may have suggested to Friedrich Schlegel the idea of his celebrated *Athenäum* fragment no. 53: "It is equally deadly for the mind to have and not to have a system. It will probably have to decide therefore to combine the two."[12] Novalis' concern about form and organization thus reflects his skepticism about the value of "watertight" systems: "Science is only one half, faith is the other" (II, 257). He was to reaffirm this view later in the form of—a notation to Kant's famous sentence, "I had to abolish knowledge in order to make room for faith."[13] Whereas for Fichte the incompleteness of the empirical self demanded that we strive for the infinite perfection and self-consistency of the pure self, for Novalis this ineluctable limitation was also a reminder for man to be humble and to submit to powers beyond the self. For him, as for the whole Romantic generation, the Spinozistic surrender of the self to the infinite powers of nature was an admirably heroic "dogmatist" stance (in Fichte's sense of the word). Whereas Fichte exalted the self, Spinoza offered a pantheist metaphysics in which man's lack of freedom was compensated for by a sense of cosmic integration. From the beginning, Novalis felt that the dialectic opposition of Spinoza's determinism and Fichte's gospel of freedom had to be synthesized, for personal as well as philosophic reasons. His exploration of the concepts God, nature, and self in the Fichte studies culminates, therefore, in the succinct key statement: "Spinoza ascended to Nature, Fichte to the Ego or the Person, I to the thesis, God" (II, 157). Much of Novalis' philosophy and theology is an elaboration on this remark, which ultimately leads to a Christian reconciliation of freedom and necessity. He could regard the Fichtean self-assertion as ethical action, but loving acquiescence to the way of things was just as moral to him, and deeply rooted in his disposition. Toward the end of his life, surrender became dominant: in the thrall of the Fichte studies, he advised his ailing brother to overcome his physical suffering through moral courage and a belief in the "universality" of his ego (IV, 172), but during his own suffering a few years later he noted: "The Lord's will be done—not mine. [. . .] Patience and surrender to the will of God are the best remedies" (IV, 57). As early as the summer of 1796, he wrote to Friedrich Schlegel that although Fichte had provided him with stimulation and intellectual excitement, he was no longer following any single preceptor; his love for Sophie defined his place in the world and gave him an ever keener feeling that all things are "sublime members of a marvellous totality," a totality which was to become "the shell" of his ego. The conclusion of the letter explicitly identifies the existential shift with a preference for Spinoza's "intellectual love for God," which was to integrate the self into the "shell," over Fichtean self-expansion:

Spinoza and Zinzendorf investigated the infinite idea of love and they had an inkling of the method [of] how on this speck of dust they could develop themselves for it, and it for themselves. It is a pity that I see nothing as yet of this perspective in Fichte, nothing of this creative breath. But he is close to it, he must step into their magic circle unless his previous life wiped the dust off his wings. (IV, 188)

The concluding metaphor contains two ironic suggestions: Fichte may have lost the dust of humanity while soaring as pure ego, or he may be unable to be a butterfly for lacking the "dust" of inspirational love. The devastating witticism written during the euphoria of Novalis' engagement is not a general denigration of philosophy in face of life; the "infinite idea of love" is itself a philosophical concept of cosmic harmony that stands in opposition to the Fichtean call to subjugate the world and the physicality of man himself. According to Novalis, nature and man's own sensuality were not to be defeated but accepted, for matter was infused with varying degrees of spirituality. Reacting to Fichte, he attempted therefore to recognize man's roots in nature (in the "not I") rather than his separation from, and opposition to, it. His position is well summarized in the pointed remarks—"I=not I—highest principle of all science and art" (II, 542) and "Thou instead of not I" (III, 430)—remarks which were echoed in Friedrich Schlegel's later demand that the not I be replaced by "a counterego, a thou."[14] I shall elaborate on these statements in my discussion of Schelling's philosophy.

Toward the end of 1796, Novalis' response to Fichte became significantly affected by his renewed friendship with Friedrich Schlegel. Until his departure for Berlin in June 1797, Schlegel was preoccupied with Fichte. His thorough study of speculative philosophy in 1796 resulted in a critique of Fichte, but when he became his friend and attended his lectures the following spring, he did not have the courage to show his critical notes. His letters to Novalis indicate that by refraining from attacks on Fichte he came to feel he was insincere (IV, 478, 482, 484–86). Only on the eve of his departure for Berlin was he able to reconcile his personal admiration for Fichte with the intellectual disagreement which by now had acquired a mellower tone and a proper role within his development (IV, 487).

Schlegel's fascination and struggle with Fichte drew Novalis once more into Fichte's "magic circle," even though Schlegel's preoccupations often seemed trivial to him amidst his own concerns for Sophie and Erasmus. In December and January, the friends engaged in long discussions that Schlegel fondly came to remember as *Fichtisieren*—that is, philosophizing in Fichte's manner. On January 1, 1797, Novalis returned Schlegel's philosophical notebooks with the remark that they had dug "rough nests" in his head (IV, 193). These impulses from Schlegel, as well as new publications by Fichte which restated his ideas with greater clarity, encouraged Novalis to prepare new notes on Fichte's philosophy, most of which unfortunately do not survive. The extant manuscripts contain excerpts and summaries which indicate a clearer but perhaps cooler view of Fichte's philosophy than the former, critically engaged studies.[15] Nor is there much evidence that "the joy of finding the actual meaning of the Fichtean Ego" (IV, 42), recorded in Novalis' diary on May 29, 1797, resulted in a renewed intellectual bondage to Fichte. Letters to Schlegel from the second half of that year suggest rather the contrary. On June 14, he reported that thanks to hints from Friedrich's "free and critical mind," he had found his way through "this terrible convolution of abstractions," thereby freeing himself "from the most dangerous of all thinkers" who immobilized everyone in his charmed circle. Friedrich was ideally suited to protect aspiring independent thinkers from "Fichte's magic" (IV, 230).

During Novalis' next visit to Fichte, the philosopher disagreed with the poet but criticized him in a mild manner (IV, 236): the apprenticeship was now over, and Novalis' intellectual emancipation allowed for the retention of mutual respect and personal admiration. Fichte remained the "president" of that philosophical directorate which included Baader, Schelling, Hülsen, and Friedrich Schlegel (II, 529), even though his philosophy "was still so stiff and timid" (III, 445). The time for surpassing Fichte in Fichtean philosophizing (*Fichtisieren*) was approaching (II, 524).

However he may have disagreed with Fichte on specific points, Novalis could claim that by departing from the literal meaning of his philosophy, he was remaining true to its spirit, for Fichte himself claimed that the fundamental ideas of his *Wissenschaftslehre* had to be understood by each student independently, through an imaginative grasp of their spirit. In the manner of Nietzsche's Zarathustra, Fichte rejected followers and demanded that creative disciples carry his message of freedom by departing from the letter of his teaching. Novalis appropriately responded by recognizing in Fichte "a call for autonomous action" (II, 271), a message he came to portray in his fictional teacher-apprentice relationships. In *Die Lehrlinge zu Sais (The Novices at Sais)*, for instance, the hero of the inserted tale, Hyazinth, burns his mentor's book in order to carry out its message.

Paradoxically, Novalis departed from Fichte by acknowledging the limitations on freedom, the dependency on forces larger than the self. He came to see that the theater of action for human freedom was not life at large, where physical infirmity and social custom were so evidently restrictive, but art, where each creative act symbolically reenacted the archetypal "intellectual intuition" and fore-shadowed a utopian state of freedom. In this sense, Novalis, like the other Romantics reacting to Fichte, reinterpreted Fichte's eth-ical striving to overcome nature as a call to find free expression in art, but this was as much a resigned recognition of limitations as it was a further exaltation of the self. The ethical imperatives of Kant and Fichte, established in reference to a transindividual pure ego, amount to "philosophies of compulsion" (IV, 181) because they de-manded the suppression of personal desires and appetites. As Schle-gel remarked, Fichte's philosophy was not "liberal" enough (IV, 482).

II *Kant*

Although Novalis must have become acquainted with Kant's phi-losophy early, his first and only extant notes pertaining to it date from 1797. Curiously, Novalis and the other Romantics studied Kant's epistemology and moral philosophy rather than the aesthetics contained in the first part of the *Kritik der Urteilskraft (Critique of Judgment)*: his notes (II, 385–94) on the Introduction and the Preface to the second edition of the *Kritik der reinen Vernunft (Critique of Pure Reason)*, the *Metaphysische Anfangsgründe der Naturwissenschaft (Metaphysical Foundations of Natural Science)*, and *Die Metaphysik der Sitten (Metaphysics of Morals)*, relate to his studies of Fichte and Hemsterhuis, but they point toward a theory of creativity all his own.

According to Kant, human knowledge is not absolute, but de-pendent on the particular structure of the mind; only the principles of action are determined, so Kant believed, by the unconditioned absolute postulates of morality. While Novalis accepted much of Kant's argument, he attempted in different ways to overcome the radical distinction between knowing and doing which emerged from it. I shall consider four of these.

Kant regarded mathematics and pure science as "forms of external sensibility" and believed that a corresponding science of "internal sensibility"—that is, a psychology—was impossible.[16] Novalis re-sponded by asking "what science concerned the forms of inner sensibility" (II, 390), and in many of his notes and fragments, he attempted what Wilhelm Dilthey was to call a *Realpsychologie*—that is, a psychology which undertakes the task of ordering the psyche's content, of grasping it in its interconnections, and as far as possible, explaining it.[17] Novalis included in this content not only the representations that our mind produces, but also the will and the emotions, anticipating thereby Schopenhauer and Nietzsche.

Kant believed that the search for the unconditioned absolute drove us beyond all limits of experience, for firm knowledge about such pure concepts of speculative reason as God, world, and freedom was impossible. In sharp contrast to Kant's (and Fichte's) theory of knowledge, Novalis believed that knowledge that does not come through the senses was possible by "stepping outside ourselves" in the kind of ecstatic self-abandonment he himself had experienced. Hence his probing response to Kant: "Is there nonsensible knowledge? Is there another way open to abandon ourselves and to reach other beings, or to be affected by them?" (II, 390). His metaphysical as well as practical answer was that love was such a way.

According to Kant, mathematics offered the paradigm of synthetic a priori knowledge, of knowledge that can grow without recourse to experience, because here pure concepts were given concrete, "constructed" images. Novalis sharpened Kant's thesis to read "Mathematical thinking multiplies itself" (II, 386), and he effectively closed the gap between knowledge and action by postulating that we may fully know and understand only those things we create: "We know only inasmuch as we fabricate" (*machen*) (II, 378 and 589). Similarly, in response to Kant's remark that the rational concept of the unconditioned can only be determined by practical reason,[18] Novalis noted: "we recognize [the unconditioned] only inasmuch as we make it real" (II, 386). Giambattista Vico had taken such a view earlier, but the statement gains special significance in the context of Romantic poetics. *Machen* is for Novalis a creative shaping and fabrication rather than simple action; hence he can ask whether the "practical" and the "poetic" could be related, the latter being merely the extreme form of the former (II, 390). In this sense, the autonomous activity of the Kantian "genius" becomes for Novalis a model for action, and he can restate the Kantian question whether synthetic a priori judgments are possible in the form: "Is there an art of invention without [given] data, an absolute art of invention?" "Is genius possible?" (III, 388). In sum, Novalis radicalizes the Kantian view of the mind's activity from a Fichtean idealist perspective, and ultimately adopts it within the framework of his poetics.

Fichte's notion that the not I was posited by the pure self took its cue from Kant's assertion that "reason recognizes only what it produces according to its own blueprint."[19] Novalis controverts this position, for as we have seen in his reaction to Fichte, he finds reason in the observed object as well as the observing subject: "Reason understands nature only inasmuch as the latter is reasonable—and henceforth agrees with it" (II, 386). This position is not incompatible with Kant's, although it gives special weight to the metaphysical assumption underlying Kant's theory—namely, that the possibility of science presupposes a rational structure for nature. The same subtle shift is evident in Novalis' rewriting of Kant's "I had to limit knowledge in order to make room for faith" to read "Where knowledge stops faith begins" (II, 387). While it is possible to read this passage Kant's way, the subsequent remark—"faith construction—construction through assumptions"—suggests that Novalis' real intention was to bring together what Kant clinically isolated: faith (metaphysical assumptions) underlies all scientific knowledge and is, in turn, a construct of the mind, different in degree, but not in kind, from everything else our mind produces. It will be well to remember that this was written a few months after Novalis had "constructed" his own faith from his psychic ruins.

III *Hemsterhuis and Baader*

François Hemsterhuis[20] achieved an unusual role in late eighteenth-century German thought, mainly through the mediating efforts in the 1780s of the Princess Gallitzin and her "Münster Circle," which included Friedrich Heinrich Jacobi and Johann Georg Hamann. The princess, a long-time Platonic friend and student of Hemsterhuis, introduced him to Goethe, Herder, and Wieland and helped to disseminate his epistles and Socratic dialogues. Hemsterhuis was a humanist with a keen sense of style, who pleaded that intuition, feeling, and the "moral organ" be reinstituted in their rightful place after having been exiled during the heyday of the enlightenment. His religious disposition paved the way toward the Romantic religious revival though it had no ties with traditional Christian beliefs.

Hemsterhuis and Plato were already Novalis' favorite philosophers in 1792 when he spoke to Friedrich Schlegel with "wild fire" about Hemsterhuis' ideas that evil didn't exist and that the golden age was to return (IV, 572). He devoted himself to a careful study of Hemsterhuis just prior to his departure for Freiberg, between September 5 and November 30, 1797, and it is from the resultant notes (II, 360–78) that I shall single out a few central ideas which had lasting impact on Novalis' intellectual development. The longest and most important work of Hemsterhuis, his *Lettre sur l'homme* (*Letter on Man*, 1772), was of greatest interest to Novalis mainly because of the concept of the "organe moral," a moral organ conceived in analogy to the senses. If we experience the visible world with our senses, we must also be endowed, according to Hemsterhuis, with a moral organ to experience the unseen "moral" world. The notion must have appealed to Novalis, who was at the time struggling to remain sensitive to Sophie's memory.

Hemsterhuis believed that man gradually perfected his intellect and senses, but allowed his moral organ progressively to atrophy. The harmonious development of man that Hemsterhuis envisioned in his dialogue *Simon ou des facultés de l'âme* (*Simon, or the Faculties of the Soul*, 1782) demanded that the moral organ be fostered and that, next to reason and logic, enthusiasm, intuition, and love also be accepted as modes of relating to the world. He sketched the utopian stage of the development in *Alexis ou de l'âge d'or* (*Alexis, or the Golden Age*, 1787), asserting that the golden age was at the eschatological endpoint of history and not at its beginning— a "truly prophetic" insight, as Novalis remarked (II, 562).

For all his insistence that the nonrational faculties be allowed to resume their role in human conduct, Hemsterhuis was neither an irrationalist nor an enemy of science. He attacked French materialism and atheism, for he considered them to be incompatible with humanism, but he had a great admiration for mathematics and pleaded for a universal science, both of which had a significant impact on Novalis' scientific studies and encyclopedia project. Hemsterhuis divided knowledge into direct, sensory knowledge and combinatorial knowledge—that is, knowledge of interrelations. He regarded the former as inferior to the latter, because in his opinion, knowledge of isolated empirical facts does not make a "savant," while insight into all the combinatorial relations was an attribute of God. Accordingly, Hemsterhuis believed that the "greatest truths of our age" were generated by the development of the sciences that dealt with pure relations—namely, geometry and arithmetic. While Diderot was uneasy with Hemsterhuis' subordination of empirical facts to abstract knowledge,[21] Novalis considered it to be a corrective to the atomism of the encyclopedists and an alternative to their way of unifying the sciences. He noted: "The sciences are separated only because of a lack of genius and keenness of mind; their relations are too complex and far-ranging for mere intellect and dull wit. We owe the greatest truths of our age to such combinations among the long separated members of total science" (II, 368). It indicates the persistence of this idea that Novalis entered it later almost verbatim into his encyclopedia notes, adding to it, in the terminology of mathematics, the reunification of the sciences will necessitate combinatorial analysis (III, 275).

Hemsterhuis' sensitivity to style and his occasional bursts into rhapsody and dithyramb showed Novalis that it was possible to write poetically about philosophy and science, while the "Socratic" poetry of Hemsterhuis' dialogues[22] pointed toward the fictional use of philosophic dialogue which Novalis later adopted. On the negative side, Hemsterhuis' Platonic conception of love, and his Spinozistic subservience to fate and the world were ultimately too passive alternatives to Fichte. But Fichte and Hemsterhuis complemented each other, and Novalis selectively took from each whatever he could incorporate into his own world view.

Novalis probably read Franz von Baader's *Beiträge zur Elementar-Phisiologie (Contributions to Physiology as a Basic Science,* 1797) before he left for Freiberg, but Baader's real impact he felt during his scientific studies in Freiberg. He enthusiastically recommended to Friedrich Schlegel that Baader, whom he did not know personally, be included in the Romantic circle, because only Friedrich could match him, and because, in the words of Schiller's "Ode to Joy," his "magic" would reunite "what stupidity's sword had severed" (IV, 263). Upon reading Baader's new essay *Ueber das pythagoräische Quadrat in der Natur (On the Pythagorean in Nature,* 1798), he had to admit that its "rough solid poetry" was "scattered over a tough mountainous terrain and [was] difficult to hew out and purify" (IV, 273), but he remained sympathetic to Baader for three major reasons: Baader envisioned the universe as an interaction of dynamic forces rather than a rigid edifice; he passionately rejected Kant's separation of facts from value and natural determinism from moral freedom; and finally, he considered love to be the bond between man, nature, and God, hence also the highest attractive force within the universe.

These views were products of the kind of synthesizing mind that appealed to Novalis. Yet it is hardly accidental that no notes on the works of Baader survive; it is likely that none were ever written. The "tough mountainous terrain" of Baader's prose, enough to scare off all but the most dedicated climbers and spelunkers, held no rare treasures. The idea of dynamic forces was already central to Herder's theory of nature; a polemic with Kantian categorization had already been undertaken by Novalis himself, who emerged from it with a theory of creativity rather than with a religious moralism resembling Baader's. Finally, with regard to love, Novalis could better appreciate Hemsterhuis' more poetic prose and his own hard-won ideas. Thus, Baader became a comrade-in-arms rather than a great mentor.

IV Schelling

The young Schelling was as indebted to Fichte as Novalis, but his admiration for Spinoza's pantheism soon caused him to develop the principles of *Naturphilosophie* which profoundly affected the direction of German science during the first decades of the nineteenth century. Schelling's *Naturphilosophie* started from the unconditional and unprovable postulate that nature and mind *(Geist)* were of a primeval identity and set out to reconstruct and regain that original identity in the mind by demonstrating that nature had the structure of consciousness: "Nature is to become visible mind, and mind invisible nature. Here then, in the absolute identity of mind within us and nature around us must the problem be resolved how external nature is possible."[23] Thus, Schelling's response to Fichte was similar to Novalis': by attempting to show systematically the omnipresence of consciousness in nature, he wished to turn the "not I" into a "Thou."

Some of the Romantics and many of their critics are guilty of trivializing this "spiritualization of nature," by interpreting it variously as anthropomorphism, animism, an instance of pathetic fallacy, or simply as a regression to a primitive understanding of the world based on feeling and intuition alone. But the introduction of elfs, sprites, or dryads into literature as relics of a perhaps happier past has little to do with Schelling's and Novalis' philosophic concerns, which for all their weaknesses, anticipate some important notions of modern science. Kant claimed that there could be no science if nature was not rational, and Fichte unwittingly agreed by asserting that the not I was posited by the pure ego and therefore somehow related to it. Schelling and Novalis relied on these assumptions and set out to discover nature's consciousness, to "win nature back" from its banishment as mere object. The gradual process of cognition was for them literally a re-cognition, a discovery of a consciousness "out there" as the foundation of nature's laws. As science progresses, nature will gradually reveal its idealistic design and lose its "mere object" quality, so that the affinity between object and subject will become evident.

The principal aim of *Naturphilosophie* was to find an a priori metaphysical principle which would allow for a "deduction" of science—that is, a systematic organization and account of empirically observed facts. Schelling thought he had found such a principle in the interaction of attractive and repulsive forces. Starting with gravity and centrifugality, he established a hierarchy of bipolar forces, which included electricity, magnetism, and organic sensibility, in order to demonstrate the unity underlying nature's apparent profusion.

Schelling's proposal to deduce science from a priori principles had such devasting effects on early nineteenth-century German science that historians today tend to overlook Schelling's contribution to the idea of nature's systematicity. *Naturphilosophie* was the formative idea behind Oersted's discovery of electromagnetism in 1821, and the notion that the profusion of natural laws must be reducible to a handful of fundamental ones is still a guiding principle of science. Among Schelling's contemporaries, Goethe also attributed dual forces to the life of nature and society, and he was therefore eager to cooperate with Schelling. But soon he became disillusioned and critical of *Naturphilosophie* because he recognized that Schelling and his disciples were all too eager to force all empirical evidence into a system.

The idea of fundamental polar forces appealed to Novalis as well, who was more inclined toward abstract philosophizing than Goethe. After reading Schelling's major works during the summer of 1797, on his way to Freiberg he visited Schelling to express his admiration for Schelling's universal bent but also to criticize his achievements so far (IV, 242). Later, especially in the extensive annotated excerpts from Schelling's *Weltseele (World Soul)* that he prepared in the late summer of 1798 (III, 102–14), he turned even more critical. Schelling asserted that the principles of transcendental philosophy did not allow for an explanation of the interaction between mind and body and concluded that philosophers should turn from empirical observations to the question of how the mind functions according to its immanent principles, while physicists should limit their attention to the physiology of life, leaving the synthetization of observation to the philosophers.[24] Novalis vehemently objected to the denial of a possible interaction between mind and body (III, 114); to the separation of science from philosophy, he ironically commented in a dialogue: "Just because we are philosophers we need not worry about the execution. We have the principle and that suffices; we leave the execution to the common minds" (II, 670). His general conclusions are well captured in a letter written to Caroline Schlegel in September 1798: "The more I grasp the immaturity of Schelling's World Soul, the greater interest I take in his mind, which divines the highest and merely lacks that gift of representation which makes Goethe the most remarkable physicist of our age. Schelling grasps well, he retains more poorly, and he is least able to reproduce" (IV, 261). Thus, Goethe was the great scientist for being able to represent and reproduce, while Schelling hastily speculated and forced the available data into overambitious schemes. Hence Schelling's ideas aged quickly. Novalis' criticism was reasonable, though he himself was not quite innocent of excessive and hasty speculation about nature, and it is curious to note that Schelling reportedly accused Novalis of "frivolity" against objects, of "sniffing around all of them without penetrating any."[25]

The differences related to substance as well as method. Schelling's World Soul was a spirit hovering between the polarities of nature—an immanent rather than transcendent spiritual power. Novalis believed that science should start with an *infinitinome* (a unit with infinite number of terms) rather than a *binome*, a polarity (III, 432)[26]: the basis of science must not be dualism, but the infinite plenitude of a divine mind encompassing nature. In response to Schelling's pantheism, he could therefore say, "God has nothing to do with nature" (III, 250) or ask, in a lighter vein, "Am I going to place God or the World Soul into heaven?" (III, 250). The disagreements finally surfaced when Schelling responded to Novalis' *Die Christenheit oder Europa (Christendom or Europe)* with the

materialist satire, *Heinz Widerporsten*. It should be added, however, that Schelling emerges from Novalis' correspondence in an
excessively negative light, due to the "group dynamics" of the Romantic circle. Novalis could hardly have been more positive about
Schelling when Friedrich Schlegel was envious of the philosopher's
success (IV, 488, 492) and August Wilhelm had to concede his wife
to Schelling in 1800.

V *Blütenstaub*

On February 24, 1798, Novalis sent off a now lost manuscript to
August Wilhelm Schlegel, commenting that it contained fragments
that were conceived earlier and had been "merely dusted off" (IV,
251). The collection, which was published in the Schlegels' Journal
Athenäum, grew out of Novalis' philosophical studies and launched
his publishing career. The years of apprenticeship in philosophy
were now essentially over; while Novalis continued to take a keen
interest in philosophy, from now on he was mainly concerned about
its application to science, poetry, and religion.

Apprenticeship and education were indeed among the important
topics of *Blütenstaub,* which Novalis gleaned from his preoccupation
with Goethe and his *Wilhelm Meister.* Goethe was for Novalis the
"true stadholder of the poetic spirit on earth" (II, 466), for he possessed a "lofty style of representation," an ability to link insignificant
events to important ones, and a talent to portray matters of which
he had no personal experience (II, 423ff.). Though *Blütenstaub*
contains only high praise for Goethe and his *Wilhelm Meister,* its
concept of education involves a Goethean integration into society
only to the extent this is necessary to gain personal freedom: "Apprenticeship in the primary sense, is apprenticeship in the art of
life. Through systematically arranged experiments, one learns life's
basic rules and acquires the facility to follow them freely" (II, 413).
Blütenstaub also shows the traces of Novalis' readings in Kant,
Fichte, Schelling, and Hemsterhuis. Some of the fragments were
directly lifted from his notes on Kant and Hemsterhuis, while others
represent combinations of and variations on his readings. The opening remark, "We seek everywhere the unconditioned *(Unbedingte)*
and find always merely things *(Dinge)*" (II, 413) is for instance an
untranslatable pun on *Ding* and *unbedingt,* concepts that are crucial
for Kant and Schelling.[27]

Novalis gave the Schlegels a free hand to do with the collection whatever they saw fit. Friedrich decided to publish the "delightful" fragments as a single unit, but an extant earlier version of the text (entitled "*Vermischte Bermerkungen*"—"Miscellaneous Remarks") tells us that he introduced significant changes. Since Novalis could also have made changes in the "Vermischte Bemerkungen", the extent of Schlegel's intervention cannot be known; but we know for certain that Friedrich Schlegel transferred thirteen fragments into his own *Athenäum-Fragmente*, added to *Blütenstaub* four of his own fragments, and cut up or telescoped several others—all this in the spirit of their *Symphilosophie* (IV, 491). The further fragmentation of Novalis' fragments had the unwelcome effect of masking the continuity of Novalis' thought and of giving his notes an air of exaggerated whimsicality and mystery. To make things worse, the collection was not republished as a unit until 1901, because Schlegel and subsequent editors dispersed the *Blütenstaub* fragments among other notes which were neither shaped nor intended for publication. Yet a proper understanding of the collection must include an appreciation of Novalis' concern with his medium and his audience.

Form of expression was an important topic in the exchanges between Schlegel and Novalis during 1797. Schlegel published that year in the *Lyceum der schönen Künste* fragments which he characterized as *kritische Chamfortade* (IV, 491) for their indebtedness to Nicolas-Sebastian Roche de Chamfort, author of witty and graceful aphorisms in the French tradition. About the same time, Schlegel became familiar with the philosophical conception of wit in the Leibnizian tradition, which assigned to that faculty the task of revealing universal harmony through the perception of analogies between apparently disparate phenomena. Schlegel fused the notions of social and philosophical wit, by considering social conversation as an occasion to show off one's brilliant wit and to gain philosophical insights. Since he no longer believed in the possibility of comprehensive and consistent systems in the great rationalist tradition, he searched for a mode of expression which acknowledged the inevitable insufficiency of human knowledge and yet pointed toward a higher unity through its own form. These considerations led him to his famous *Athenäum* fragment no. 206: "Like a small work of art, a fragment must be completely detached from the surrounding world, and complete in itself like a hedgehog."[28] Although the *Athenäum* fragments appeared after the publication of *Blütenstaub*,

Schlegel surely discussed his notion of the fragment with Novalis, and these conversations must have played a formative role in Novalis' thinking on the subject. Wit, "the product of imagination and judgment" (II, 425), actually became a recurrent subject of *Blütenstaub.* It was for Novalis a sign of "disturbed equilibrium" (Schlegel wrote later that wit revealed the fragmentariness of human existence), because serene minds were not witty (II, 429): "As a principle of connections, wit is simultaneously the 'menstruum universale' [the universal solvent of the alchemists]" (II, 435).

The solving and bonding power of wit is social and artistic as well as intellectual. A true club, to cite one of Novalis' examples, would bring all three aspects together: it would be a social institution with an aesthetic design, having no other purpose but to offer occasions to chat freely and to use the topics as mere "means of animation". The bonding power of wit turns a social company into "an indivisible, thinking and feeling person. Each person is a little company" (II, 429ff.).

Precisely because Novalis adopted in these fragments Friedrich's notion of wit, he could not agree with Schlegel that fragments had to be self-contained and finished: "Whoever intends to take fragments of this sort literally may be an honorable man—but he should not consider himself a poet. Must one always be circumspect?" (II, 466). Although this fragment from "Vermischte Bemerkungen" was not included in the published version, its message became incorporated into the closing fragment of *Blütenstaub:* "Fragments of this sort are literary seeds. Of course there may be some sterile kernels among them—but if only a few will take!" (II, 463). This in turn explicates the motto of the collection:

> Friends, the soil is poor, rich seeds we must sow
> To grow even a mediocre harvest! (II, 413)

The "poor soil"—that is, the paucity of good books and the low intellectual demand of the audience—justifies the pollination and seeding. The art of writing books has not yet been invented (II, 463); most books are cheap coins or paper money—as Novalis points out in a witty extended metaphor (II, 457). Elsewhere he compares reviewers with physicians and asks that they not only enforce codes and cure diseases but practice *medizinische Polizei*—namely, preventive medicine and public health as demanded in a historically important book by Johann Peter Frank (II, 464).

The inefficiency of communication, to which Schlegel gives no attention, leads to Novalis' notion that fragments must be tentative. Both as pollen and as seed, the fragmentary utterance is part of an organic cycle where one finds waste and sterility as much as organic growth. The creative mind is a pollen which has to reach the pistil or a seed which needs fertile soil to germinate and grow. A receptive audience is paramount: "The true reader must be an extended author. He is the higher instance that receives the matter from the lower instance in prepared form" (II, 470). This remark echoes Fichte's demand for creative reception and a comment Novalis made on Hemsterhuis: "The letter of the alphabet is only an aid in philosophic communication, whose actual essence consists of reconsideration *(Nachdenken)*. [. . .] Words are an unreliable medium for aiding the thoughts of others *(Vordenken)*. Genuine truth must, by nature, point the way" (II, 373). Hence the pen name Novalis, adopted for the publication of *Blütenstaub* for the first time, was "not entirely unfitting" (IV, 251) in a double sense: the poet was clearing uncultivated, fallow land (a twelfth century branch of the family called itself de Novali=from the rodeland), first in the intellectual sense of opening up new fields of inquiry, and second in that he wanted to educate an audience which was as yet unable to respond creatively to artistic and intellectual stimulation.

But the "mystic expression" (II, 485) of the fragments cut both ways: on the one hand it was to tease the reader's mind, on the other it indicated a desire to communicate with select initiates only. Novalis' next collection, *Glauben und Liebe (Faith and Love)*, rather arrogantly addressed itself only to those who already possessed the key to the secret language (II, 488). Just, who suspected that the remarks about incomprehending philistines were directed against him, admonished Novalis for being a "friend of antitheses" in order to appeal to the witty minds of the young and decided to take up the cause of the common reader:

One must have some familiarity with your language in order to understand and judge you. I believe I know your language and turn of mind better than most of your readers, yet much has remained inexplicable to me in the fragments. Therefore I wish [. . .] you would, in the future, show greater respect for the audience, so that they read you more, understand you better, and judge you more justly. Retain forever your originality of thought and wealth of images, but use a more comprehensible language.

For as soon as you write *in* public you must also write *for* the public. Or do you wish to write for a few initiates only? (IV, 506)

Just was of course right: the Schlegelian apprentice was all too eager to speak the language of initiates. Novalis could only reply that he meant to stimulate: the fragments were merely "starters for interesting trains of thought, texts for thought. Many of them are counters *(Spielmarken)* and have only transitory value." (IV, 270f.). Just's comments may have played a role in Novalis' later deliberate attempts to communicate poetically to a larger audience. The adoption of his devotional songs in hymnals is a measure of his success.

A careful examination of the central *Blütenstaub*-fragments reveals, however, that even at this stage, Novalis did not aristocratically scorn the common man, whom he distinguished from the philistine, the petit bourgeois. The sharp attack on philistinism in the seventy-seventh fragment charges the philistines with a trivialization of religious visions in terms of social conceptions. Novalis' scathing irony anticipates Marx's analysis of the social uses of religion: the philistines use religion as an "opiate" to assuage the pains of daily life and to assure themselves a future commensurate with their present social status; the coarse philistines "imagine the joys of heaven in the picture of a kermes, a wedding, a journey, or a ball," while the finer, "more sublime" philistines "turn heaven into a magnificent church with beautiful music, much pageantry, with seats for the common folk in the parterre and chapels and choirs for the prominent" (II, 447). While Novalis attacks the unimaginative philistines, he defends the "common folk in the parterre," the average guy, against "recent abuses," by asking whether steady mediocrity does not require the greatest force and whether man should be more than just one of the "popolo" (II, 431).

The philistines know only their everyday life and have become estranged from their essential self, forgetting that man is not merely a common sense being, but by virtue of his "higher self," also citizen of an invisible order. This "higher self" is neither inaccessible, as with Kant, nor accessible by cogitation only, as with Fichte, but directly available through intuition: "The most unfounded misconception is that man doesn't have the ability to be outside himself, to be consciously out of his senses. Man is capable of becoming any moment an extrasensuous being. Without this he would not be a citizen of the world but an animal" (II, 421). The central message of *Blütenstaub* is that man has to reawaken his lost intuition and overcome his self-alienation, not only for his own sake, but to "save" nature: "We are on a mission. To mold the earth is our calling" (II, 427). Everyday life demands so much energy and perseverance perhaps only "because nothing is more uncommon for a genuine human being than paltry ordinariness" (II, 416). While the here and now is indispensible, the invisible world is more accessible: "The highest is most comprehensible, the nearest most indispensible. Only unfamiliarity with our own self, alienation *(Entwöhnung)* from ourselves, can give rise to an incomprehension which is itself incomprehensible" (II, 416). Restated in Fichtean terminology: "The highest goal of education is to take possession of one's transcendental self, to reach the self of one's self" (II, 425). This can, of course, never be achieved in purely rational ways: "We shall never fully comprehend ourselves, but we shall, and we are able to, achieve much more than comprehension" (II, 413). As the famous sixteenth fragment states, self-knowledge is reached over "the secret path" to inwardness:

Die Fantasie setzt die künftige Welt entweder in die Höhe, oder in die Tiefe, óder in der Metempsychose zu uns. Wir träumen von Reisen durch das Weltall: ist denn das Weltall nicht in uns? Die Tiefen unsers Geistes kennen wir nicht.—Nach Innen geht der geheimniβvolle Weg. In uns, oder nirgends ist die Ewigkeit mit ihren Welten, die Vergangenheit und Zukunft. Die Auβenwelt ist die Schattenwelt, sie wirft ihren Schatten in das Lichtreich. Jetzt scheint es uns freilich innerlich so dunkel, einsam, gestaltlos, aber wie ganz anders wird es uns dünken, wenn diese Verfinsterung vorbei, und der Schattenkörper hinweggerückt ist. Wir werden mehr genieβen als je, denn unser Geist hat entbehrt. (II, 417ff.)
(Imagination sets afterlife either high up, or in the depth, or in metempsychosis. We dream about journeys through the cosmos—is the cosmos not within us? We do not know the profundities of our spirit. Inward leads the secret path. In us or nowhere is eternity with its past and future worlds. The external world is a world of shadows, it casts its shadow into the realm of light. Now it appears to us so dark, lonely, and shapeless inside; but how very different will it seem to us when this eclipse is over and the shadowing body is removed. We shall enjoy more than ever, for our spirit has known privation.)

This is the great theme of Novalis' *Hymnen an die Nacht*, anticipation also of Rilke's "Nowhere, beloved, can world exist but within,"[29] albeit still coupled with a genuine belief in afterlife. Both for Rilke and for Novalis the inward path terminates in death, but for Novalis, death is a point of commutation: if life was the sleep of the genuine self, death is the "escape of the spirit of mediocrity" (II, 451) and rebirth of the real self: "Death is a conquest over the self which, like all self-overcoming, creates a new, lighter existence" (II, 414).

CHAPTER 3

Apprenticeship in Science

I At the Freiberg Mining Academy

AS early as 1791, Novalis included Franklin, Linné, Haller, Newton, and Galileo among mankind's great educators (IV, 95); but,
apart from the two week exposure to chemistry, he undertook serious scientific studies only when in the first months of 1797 philosophy aroused his interest in science. He sustained this interest
during the spring and summer of that year, hoping that science
would offer him a sense of permanence and security. In his last
letter to his dying brother, he lauded Erasmus' plan to study algebra, for "the sciences have miraculous healing powers, at least
they still pains like opiate and raise us into spheres of eternal sun-
shine" (IV, 202f.) With their aid, he hoped to weather all the ad-
versities of life. Though at the time of Sophie's death he felt that
the sciences were also "dead, barren, deaf, and immobile" (IV, 204),
they soon reassumed their significance, because now he studied
them "from a higher perspective" (IV, 215) and thereby refashioned
his tie to life (IV, 219). He later acknowledged that his "old idea
of independence and his love for some of the sciences" (IV, 287),
rather than career considerations, were foremost on his mind in
deciding to study at the Freiberg Mining Academy. Only after his
engagement to Julie Charpentier did he wish to put his scientific
knowledge to use in a career in the Saxon administration.

Freiberg was a small mining town of barely 10,000 inhabitants,
tucked away in the Saxon Erzgebirge, some thirty kilometers southwest of Dresden. Its silver mining, which started in the twelfth,
and peaked during the second half of the sixteenth, century, petered
out by the end of the eighteenth century. The founding of the
mining academy in 1765 was to help modernize technology and to

increase mining productivity, in order to refill the coffers of the Saxon treasury, which had been depleted during the Seven Years War of 1756–1763. It was a wise and far-sighted decision: Saxony established a technological institute well before France and England, both more advanced industrially and scientifically, and the venture was so successful that it acquired a worldwide reputation and eventually contributed to the rapid increase of Saxon mining productivity during the nineteenth century.

The academy established its reputation primarily through Abraham Gottlob Werner, a geologist who wrote his first and only treatise *Von den äußerlichen Kennzeichen der Foßilien (On the External Characteristics of Minerals,* 1774) while still a student in Leipzig. The following year, the book netted him the chair of mining and mineralogy in Freiberg, and soon students from all over the world flocked to hear this meticulous scholar and dedicated teacher whose encyclopedic interests included philology, classics, and military science—to name only a few. Novalis was immediately attracted to his "great systematic spirit" (IV, 298) and "divinatory insight," but he also learned from him that practical expertise which enabled him later to apply for technical positions (IV, 287). In return, he erected literary monuments to Werner in the teacher figures of his novels.

Werner had a curious career. Having established his reputation with his book, he became the celebrated father of "Neptunist" geology without ever writing a treatise on it: the theory gained currency in Germany and England through publications by his students. In contrast to the "Volcanists," who claimed that the earth's surface was molded primarily by volcanic activity, the "Neptunists" believed that rocks were deposits of a sea that once covered all of the earth's surface. The Romantics and Goethe, who incorporated the debate into Act II of *Faust II,* were Neptunists, but history ultimately proved them wrong. Werner relied excessively on data obtained in the Saxon mountains, and he insisted, without empirical evidence, that the basalt and the other volcanic rocks that geologists were busily exploring in southern France were also deposits from water.

Among those who contributed to the academy's reputation was Christlieb Ehregott Gellert, a brother of the poet and a top metallurgist, who taught there in the early years, and August Wilhelm Lampadius, who assumed the chair of chemistry in 1795. Lampadius was a prominent champion of Lavoisier's new chemistry; barely a year after his arrival, he discovered carbonic disulphide and established the world's first scientific laboratory at an institution of higher learning. In contrast, the mathematics lectures of Johann Friedrich Lempe were so poor that Novalis had to take tutorials from a fellow student.

Unlike Novalis, most of his sixty-odd fellow students followed a full three to four year course of study, paying if they were of noble descent or on scholarship if their middle class parents were in state service. Alexander von Humboldt attended Freiberg in 1791 and 1792, while subsequent classes included such prominent proponents of *Naturphilosophie* as Gotthilf Heinrich Schubert (from 1805 to 1807) and Henrik Steffens (from 1799 to 1801). Basic and applied science were interlinked at the academy. Lampadius taught, for instance, chemistry and metallurgy, while Werner lectured on mining and smelting on one hand, and on geognosy and the "Encyclopedia of Mining Science" on the other. A practicum in the mines was an integral part of the program, and scholarship students had to earn part of their support there.

Novalis arrived in Freiberg toward the end of the academic year and adjusted only gradually. He spent his first few months with intensive writing: by February 24, he had completed the "Miscellaneous Remarks" and by May 11, *Glauben und Liebe;* other fragment collections and *Die Lehrlinge zu Sais* were in the making (IV, 251). Meanwhile he undertook travels, including a trip to Weimar, where he met Schiller and the apparently ill-humored Goethe (IV, 257). At first he felt quite lonely in Freiberg and in need of intellectual conversations (IV, 243). He considered himself diligent at digesting all that "empirical rubbish," though he was happy only when he could engage in his "dear speculation": "If the empiricists give me a hard time, I'll create an empirical world of my own where everything neatly goes at the behest of a speculative slob *(Schlendrian)*" (IV, 247). He was ready to allay the fear that he might become "all a + b" in Freiberg with the promise to hold mathematics in contempt for reducing him to a tyro. As to chemistry: "my old inclination toward the absolute luckily rescued me once more from the whirlpool of empiricism, and I am floating now, and perhaps for good, in lighter and more eccentric spheres" (IV, 251).

But these jesting remarks to his fellow literati belittle the actual interest he took in science and the social adjustment he made in Freiberg. He did not reject science, he only searched for its "po--

etization." Though he missed the "electrifying conversations" with the Schlegels (IV, 251), by February he was a frequent and welcome guest in the house of Johann Friedrich Wilhelm von Charpentier, a retired professor of mathematics, who was now in the administration of the mines. Novalis enjoyed the company of his two daughters, Caroline and Julie, who would be inspired by the sermons of their "Eleusinian priest" about "future, nature, and human life" (IV, 250). Caroline had greater intellectual and artistic gifts, but Julie, who could only play the glass harmonica, was so sensitive to the delicate feelings of the poet that she seemed like "slow poison" to him, all the more dangerous for being so palatable. The venom worked slowly because it fostered not death but renewed commitment to life, which Novalis was reluctant to take upon himself: "all this is quite nice, but I am no longer the person I used to be, I no longer fit in the world" (IV, 250). His hesitation between detachment and new attachment found an appropriate image in the poem entitled "Der Fremdling" ("The Stranger"), which he wrote for the birthday of Mrs. Charpentier in January 1798:

> Müde bist du und kalt, Fremdling, du scheinest nicht
> Dieses Himmels gewohnt—wärmere Lüfte wehn
> Deiner Heimat und freier
> Hob sich vormals die junge Brust. (I, 399)

(Tired you are and cold, stranger, you don't seem to be / accustomed to this sky—warmer breezes flutter / in your homeland and your young chest heaved more freely formerly.)

Though the poet asserts that this exile "gladly lingers where he finds companions, celebrates cheerfully with you the feast of domestic joys" (I, 400), the final two stanzas increase his distance from the celebrants by separating the "poet" from his inarticulate social self and by requesting in a tone of self-pity compassion from the others:

> Dieses wünschet der Gast—aber der Dichter sagts
> Euch für ihn; denn er schweigt gern, wenn er freudig ist,
> Und er sehnet so eben
> Seine fernen Geliebten her.
> Bleibt dem Fremdlinge hold—spärliche Freuden sind
> Ihm hienieden gezählt—doch bei so freundlichen

> Menschen sieht er geduldig
> Nach dem großen Geburtstag hin. (I, 400)

(This is what the guest wishes, but the poet says it / to you for him, because he likes to be silent when he is happy / and just now he yearns for his distant beloved ones to be here.
Remain kind to the stranger—sparse joys are / allotted to him here—yet among such friendly / people he looks patiently/ forward to the great birthday.)

Novalis' great "day of birth" into the "invisible world" was barely three years away, but the remaining time was as much a reawakening to the joys of this world as it was a preparation for the other. In content and meter the poem that Novalis wrote for Mrs. Charpentier's next birthday marks the change that took place within a year:

> Der müde Fremdling ist verschwunden
> Und hat dem Freunde Platz gemacht,
> [. . .]
> Von keinem Kummer mehr bewacht
> Hat er sich wieder selbst gefunden,
> Und manches, was er nicht gedacht. (I, 405)

(The tired stranger disappeared / and made way for the friend, [. . .] no longer imprisoned by any grief / he has regained himself / and some things he did not expect.)

The secret engagement to Julie took place at Christmas 1798, at the end of an eventful year. The next summer Novalis fell ill, probably with his first bout of tuberculosis, and he had to spend four weeks at the Bohemian spa of Teplitz recuperating, writing his "Teplitz fragments" (II, 596–622), and mulling over several other projects. In August, during a two day visit to the Dresden Art Galleries with Schelling and the Schlegels, he received a lasting impression of Raphael's Sistine Madonna. As in the case of Sophie, his attachment to Julie became more intense when Julie fell ill in the second half of the year and his love mingled with compassion.

The second engagement did not come easily, for the human bondage to Julie had to be reconciled with his poetic and mystic love for Sophie; as Caroline Schlegel wittily remarked, she never knew whether Novalis was enamored with "the harmony of the worlds" or the artist of the "glass harmonica" (IV, 518). However, as Sophie gradually became a source of inspiration and practical life continued to ask for commitments, the idea of marriage became more reasonable. Novalis came to feel that for the duration of his life he had to be a useful member of society, and marriage was a means to achieve this end. His later account of the decision reflects once more an overdose of pragmatism: "I saw that without a loving helper, life and any participation in worldly affairs would [. . .] remain an oppressive burden [. . .] I knew that I could never find a more faithful, reliable, and tender spouse—felt that a [financially] limited situation would be advantageous to me by stimulating my diligence and that no other girl could be as helpful to me in enduring it" (IV, 312).

Financial problems, which were at the root of the father's temporary opposition to the marriage, now took precedence over literary plans: "penmanship is a side affair, you judge me fairly by the main thing: practical life" (IV, 266). Commercial concerns were now "the order of the day," and chemistry and technology the preferred subjects of study (IV, 270), for his "apprenticeship" was drawing to a close and the demands of domestic life asserted themselves (IV, 275). He preferred civil service to the profession of writing, but career and domestic happiness were ultimately mere foundations for a poetic life: "One has to build a poetic world around oneself and live in poetry. That is the function of my mercantile plan. To the latter I subordinate penmanship" (IV, 275).

It seemed fitting that Friedrich Schlegel's moving in with Dorothea Veith, daughter of the philosopher Moses Mendelssohn, should have opened a new phase at that point in the friend's life. While Novalis predicted little success for Schlegel's *Lucinde*, which gave a frank account of the sexual odyssey that led Friedrich into the arms of Dorothea, he saw the emergence of a new Romantic community: "Only now can there be true friendship among us, since societies consist not of individuals but of families—only families can form societies. Singles are of interest to society only as fragments and in their capacity to become family members" (IV, 278). In May 1799, Novalis left Freiberg and returned to Weißenfels in search of an administrative post and domestic happiness.

II   Wernerian Geology

Upon his return to Weißenfels, Novalis was, next to Goethe, probably the scientifically best educated poet of his age. Although he was occasionally critical of the science he studied and he often complained to his literary friends about its tedium, the sheer volume and range of his scientific notes demonstrate that he was serious about his studies and fascinated by them.

The Freiberg notebooks can be divided into three categories: (1) lecture notes and technical remarks, (2) reading notes and excerpts (III, 34–203), and (3) the "Allgemeines Brouillon" ("General Outline or Sketch", III, 242–478), a repository of sundry excerpts, reflections, and imaginative associations brought together within an encyclopedia project. The following discussion of Novalis' scientific studies shall completely omit the first category, of which only a few pages survive, and limit the account of the second to a short characterization of Novalis' reactions to Werner's classification of minerals. The principles of the encyclopedia project will be subject of the subsequent section.

Novalis' extensive notes on Werner's classification of minerals (III, 135–61) indicate his ability to perceive philosophical issues in narrow scientific subjects. Werner classified minerals by carefully inspecting their external physical features, refraining, however, from any inferences as to their chemical composition. He believed that appearance did not reveal chemical composition and that the relationship between external signs and internal structure could only be established once both were set up independently. The thrust of Novalis' criticism was that internal chemical composition and externally observable color, hardness, smell, and shape were inseparable: appearance and chemistry related to each other as signifier and signified, making geognosy a branch of semiotics. Real progress could only be made once the nature of geognostic signs and the syntax of nature's sign language were clarified; however, as he wrote in a letter, "we still miss some most important chapters in the grammar of that language of general physics, and even Werner's boldly outlined alphabet and syntax seem to have great gaps" (IV, 298). Without a semiotic foundation, Werner's classification of minerals appeared arbitrary, even though it rested on most careful and "objective" empirical observations.

I merely mention that Novalis' scientific readings in Freiberg included Pierre Simon Laplace's *Exposition du système du monde* (*Exposition of the System of the World*), F.A.C. Gren's *Grundriβ der Naturlehre* (*Outline of the Study of Nature*), Johann Heinrich Lambert's *Neues Organon* (*New Organon*), and mathematical textbooks by Charles Bossut and Friedrich Murhard, as well as books and articles on crystallography, physiology, chemistry, and physics. While his primary interest remained philosophical and theoretical, he acquired during his relatively short stay in Freiberg a competence in technical matters which he put to good use later in the administration of the salt mines and in Werner's geological survey. Immersed in practical and technical problems, he came to regret that the great physicists of his age cared so little about applied science (IV, 306).

III *Mathematics and the Encyclopedia Project*

Novalis' "Brouillon" is a collection of excerpts, notes, marginalia, and speculations established in order to gather the fields of learning in an encyclopedic project and to demonstrate thereby the coherence of knowledge. This unity of knowledge is a central topic of the "Brouillon," made evident also in the treatment of the individual subjects and in the imaginative links and associations established between them. Since the "Brouillon" contains excerpts from and commentaries on d'Alembert's *Discours préliminaire* (*Preliminary Discourse*) to the great French *encyclopédie*, the best approach to it will be via other eighteenth-century encyclopedia projects.

As stated in the *Discours préliminaire*, the epistemological principles of the French encyclopedia rely on the ideas of Bacon and Locke. Following Locke's assertion that all knowledge comes through the senses or is a product of reflection, d'Alembert distinguishes between direct and indirect knowledge; following Bacon, he ascribes direct knowledge to the faculty of memory and indirect knowledge to reason and imagination. The three faculties—memory, reason, and imagination—produce three branches of knowledge—history, philosophy, and art, respectively. D'Alembert raises the imagination above memory and reason but continues to ascribe a largely imitative function to it. Though he adopts and modifies Bacon's "tree of knowledge" in this way to demonstrate the unity of all science, that scheme could not be used to order the encyclopedia's unwieldy mass of information, and the editors had to adopt an alphabetical organization which could not demonstrate the interrelation of the parts.

Novalis shared d'Alembert's belief in the unity of all knowledge (III, 356 and 364), but their verbal agreement masks underlying conceptual differences. He reorganized Bacon's scheme by making the imagination the active force *(wirkende Kraft)* of the other faculties (III, 298) and thereby posited the imagination as the synthesizing power of the encyclopedia. Novalis would have agreed with Coleridge that imagination was "the living power and prime agent of all human perception,"[1] and with Shelley that poetry was "at once the centre and circumference of knowledge."[2] But he did not attribute an organic structure to the imagination; he did not insist, as Goethe did, that the concrete image was "the momentary living revelation of the unfathomable";[3] and he did not see, as Blake did, "a world in a grain of sand."[4] Like Schiller, he was fond of abstract generalizations, and thus the flight from the "whirlpool of empiricism" led him to those spheres of mathematics where unifying principles for the encyclopedia could be found.

From Kant he learned that mathematical representations were not copies of empirical objects in the world, but images constructed from abstract concepts. We may, for instance, depict a triangle (in mind or on paper) and arrive at new insights without empirical investigations by considering its properties. The imaginary triangle, which makes the expansion of knowledge possible, must be related to shapes we encounter in the empirical world, but, so Kant would insist, it is not abstracted from them. Hence mathematics is neither an empirical science based on sense perception, nor a sister of metaphysics, the science which vainly hopes to construct indubitable knowledge from concepts to which no perceptions correspond: mathematics became for Kant the paradigm of science, and a science was genuine to him only inasmuch as it contained mathematics.[5]

Kant believed in a single "natural science," because all the genuine sciences incorporated mathematics; but, according to him, the imaginative projection (Kant uses the term "construction") of concepts into the sphere of perception was only possible in mathematics. Novalis, once again, modified what he learned: he accepted from Kant the notion that the mathematical method allowed an expansion of knowledge without recourse to experience, but he believed that this method was representative of science in general (III, 457). In direct response to the crucial passages in Kant's *Kritik der reinen Vernunft,*[6] he asserted that the embodiment of concepts in perception *(Plastisierung)* could be used in all fields of science (III, 123), because this was the function of the imagination. The question for him was not to inject mathematics into the individual sciences but to universalize the role of the imagination in mathematics. As a rule, knowledge could be generated by allowing the imagination to project images that correspond to concepts onto the screen of perception; and this method guaranteed for him the unity of knowledge—a unity which was therefore based on a "poetization" of the sciences. To put it in nontechnical terms, the unity of the encyclopedia lay for him in the universal use of the imagination.

Curiously, Novalis' encyclopedia project was equally strongly indebted to a second and completely different concept of mathematics, which was first formulated by Leibniz and later developed by Gottlob Frege, Bertrand Russell, and others into symbolic logic and logistic mathematics. According to this view, mathematical deductions do not expand knowledge because all conclusions are contained in the premises. Hence mathematics is a branch of logic: the chosen axioms determine the deducible theorems. In a way very different from Kant, Leibniz also believed that mathematics was a paradigm of all knowledge: in analogy to the division of numbers into prime components, he envisioned a reexamination of knowledge in terms of the decomposition of all complex concepts into a limited set of fundamental ones. Once that set was established and each basic concept was given a clear and unequivocal sign, all knowledge could be generated by a logical calculus or a combination of signs, and thinking became calculation. Leibniz never tackled the project systematically, but he knew that it necessitated a semiotics to designate the fundamental concepts with clear and combinable signs and two kinds of encyclopedias: one to contain all the unexamined concepts and one for those already clarified and available for a logical calculus. Since the first encyclopedia was to be the starting point of his visionary project, Leibniz made untiring but unsuccessful efforts to win the support of scientific societies and potentates. His plan for a logical calculus was neglected during the eighteenth century and declared unrealizable by Kant's followers, but Novalis was able to reconstruct its outline and utilize it for his "Brouillon" through familiarity with the work of Johann Heinrich Lambert and Carl Friedrich Hindenburg in combinatorics and logical calculus. He received additional ideas from Lessing's, Herder's, Lambert's, Moses Mendelssohn's, Fichte's, Hemsterhuis' and Condorcet's writings on the role of signs in the sciences and arts.

Semiotics *(Zeichenlehre)* is a central subject of the "Brouillon," because Novalis came to realize that a comparative theory of signs may be the best means of unifying the encyclopedia: designating, signifying, phenomenologizing, is the general task of the intelligent imagination. Linguistic signs are not specifically different from other signs (III, 450). Accordingly, we find in the "Brouillon" notes on the semiotics of clothing (III, 397), minerals, medical symptoms and their relation to bodily functions (III, 141), and on Lavoisier's new chemistry, which was developing its nomenclature of compounds from a combinatorics of alphabetical signs. In terms of this chemistry, Lambert's logical calculus appeared as "intellectual chemistry" (III, 422).

The foundation of a semiotics in the arts was laid by Gotthold Ephraim Lessing, who asserted in his *Laokoon* that the signs of the visual arts were spatially combined while those of poetry—namely, words—were combined temporally. This first major step toward a rapprochement between poetry and music on the grounds of their common temporality was followed by a second one taken by Novalis, who postulated a further kinship between the signs themselves: poetic signs ought to become self-contained and meaningless, like musical notes. Ultimately, such a view of poetic language asked that words be purified, cleansed from their everyday meaning; after sporadic attempts by Novalis, Tieck, and Brentano, this was, indeed, systematically carried out by the French Symbolist poets. Novalis' main contribution was to recognize that the analogy between music and the new poetry rested on the nonreferential nature of their signs. Precisely this feature brought music and poetry into the proximity of algebra. Here "empty" individual letters acquired a general meaning within a formulaic combination and became concrete whenever numerical values were substituted for them. Music and algebra were "general N-languages" (III, 283) whose combinatorial kinship is indicated, for instance, in the following "Brouillon" entry:

Musical mathematics.
Doesn't music contain some combinatorial analysis and vice versa?
Numerical-harmonies, number-acoustics belong to combinatorial analysis.
[. . .] Combinatorial analysis leads to number-fantasias and teaches the

compositional art of numbers, the mathematical cyphered base. (Pythagoras. Leibniz.) Language is a musical idea instrument. The poet, the rhetorician, and the philosopher play and compose grammatically. (III, 360)

Novalis' study of algebra (III, 167ff.) actually ran parallel to the work on the encyclopedia. The "Brouillon" was to become a "scientific algebra" containing "equations, relations, similarities, identities, and interactions" among the various sciences (III, 279f.) and could therefore be called a "combinatorial study of scientific operations" (III, 361). To be sure, Novalis did not plan to undertake the kind of logical analysis of concepts that Leibniz had envisioned, merely an *"Encyclopaedisierungscalcul"* (III, 290), a combinatorial calculus of ideas, indicated already by such titles of his entries as "physical philosophy," "musical physics," or "analogical physiology." His mind functioned as a "loom of ideas" (IV, 211), and his method consisted of an application of the "magic wand of analogy" (III, 518). This was not incompatible with the broader meaning of the Leibnizian *ars combinatoria*, which Leibniz himself had characterized as a general science of analogies, symmetries, and transformations.[7]

In one final respect, we may approach Novalis' project from a Leibnizian perspective. Mathematics in general and combinatorics specifically can represent existing things as a subset of a larger set of possible entities. Since the laws of permutation and combination allow a systematic representation of all possibilities, combinatorics contains, as Novalis remarked, the principle of completeness (III, 364). Because of its ability to represent everything logically possible, combinatorics recommends itself for the construction of a perfect encyclopedia. By aiming at the generality of a mathematical equation rather than the enumeration of empirical particulars, the Leibnizian combinatorial concept offered a more general, yet tighter, organization for the encyclopedia than the empirical principles of Bacon and Locke. Methodologically, the "Brouillon" represents a critique of empiricism in part from a perspective of Leibnizian rationalism.

For Leibniz, the real world represents that arrangement out of infinite possibilities which the supreme master of combinatorics, God, had to choose because it was "the best of all possibilities" and minimized evil. The brilliant satirization of that theory in Voltaire's *Candide* missed the point of Leibniz' argument, but it reflected the increasing dissatisfaction of the eighteenth century with the conditions of the world. The rebellion of the early German Romantics represented the last stage of that dissatisfaction where disappointment in social revolution led to a belief that only through the cultivation of the imagination could the world be ultimately changed. If, for Leibniz, the original divine creation fixed once and for all the choice among the infinite possibilities, for the Romantics the human imagination became the means to improve the world by the construction of other, better possibilities. According to the new aesthetic credo, it behooves the poet and the scientist to recast the world by the development of new imaginative combinations. The poetics that Novalis developed during the last years of his life grew, therefore, out of his studies in mathematics and his experiment with the encyclopedia. His shift from empiricism to abstract mathematical formalism parallels the epochal shift from mimetic artistic reproduction of reality to abstract verbal combinations and to representations of possible realities in poems and fairy tales.

IV   The Book

When Novalis gradually recognized the practical problems involved in the construction of the encyclopedia, he shifted his attention to problems in methodology, organization, and articulation (III, 356). The preoccupation with formal questions is evident, for instance, in a plan to send Friedrich Schlegel a sample of the encyclopedia in as "romantic" a manner as possible. It contains a catalogue of possible formats, suggesting that the "Brouillon" was meant to become an encyclopedia of styles and literary forms as well, preparing thereby the ground for the poetic works: "Should it be a recherche (or essay), a collection of fragments, a commentary in Lichtenberg's style, a report, a testimony, a story, an article, a review, a speech, a monologue, or a fragment of a dialogue?" (III, 277f.).

Based on the conviction that "all knowledge constitutes a single book" (III, 365), encyclopedias are designed to capture the macrocosm and are therefore not unlike those fictional books that appear in Novalis' Die Lehrlinge zu Sais, Heinrich von Ofterdingen, and the poem "An Tieck" ("To Tieck"), in E. T. A. Hoffmann's Der goldene Topf (The Golden Flower Pot), or in Book V (appropriately entitled "Books") of Wordsworth's Prelude, which incorporate mysterious insights into fate and nature. The romantic belief in a "book of all books" is rooted in the mystic and cabalistic traditions, pointing forward to the dream of such modern writers as Stéphane Mallarmé, James Joyce, Marcel Proust, Thomas Mann, Hermann Broch, or Robert Musil to enclose all knowledge within the covers of an encyclopedic book. Indeed, Novalis' encyclopedia project grew in an intimate symbiosis with Friedrich Schlegel's vision of a "progressive Universalpoesie" that would reunite the literary genres, fuse philosophy and literature, and saturate the arts with "all kinds of learning."[8]

Inevitably, the notion of an encyclopedic book led to reflections about the Bible, the archetypal book of the Judeo-Christian tradition: if the universe was to be encapsulated in a book, the Bible was the proper model (III, 683). Friedrich Schlegel and Novalis arrived independently at this conclusion, but they embarked upon quite dissimilar Bible projects. Schlegel had a literally religious project in mind, a modern Bible in service of a new religion, while he correctly observed that Novalis' project was more literary (IV, 507). Novalis came to regard the Bible as the ideal of all books while studying science and its embodiment in books, but his account makes the artistic interest evident: "The fully developed theory of the Bible will yield the theory of writing or word-construction in general," and this, in turn, will contain the "symbolic, indirect doctrine of construction for the creative mind." Novalis worked on a "criticism of the Bible project, an attempt to find the universal method of Bible writing, an introduction to a genuine encyclopedic project." With its aid, he hoped to generate "great truths and ideas, to produce brilliant thoughts, and to create a living scientific organon" (IV, 263). The "Brouillon" was meant to become "a scientific bible, a real and ideal model, and the seed of all books" (III, 363).

V *"Logical Physics"*

Novalis' encounter with the philosophy of Plotinus in Dietrich Tiedemann's history of speculative philosophy (IV, 269) was one of his crucial intellectual experiences in Freiberg. In Plotinus' scheme, as presented by Tiedemann, mental and physical entities were both emanations of an all-encompassing mind. The creative contemplation of that mind, symbolized by light radiating from it, produced the physical world in a hypostatisation, an arrestation of that light. For Novalis, too, the world was "a palpable, machine-turned imag-

ination" (III, 252). While Tiedemann was more appreciative of Plotinus than his eighteenth-century predecessors, he was critical of
what he considered to be Plotinus' play with words and empty
abstractions. It was all well and good to juggle words, as long as
one didn't make the mistake to assume that by combining these,
one was in any way affecting or saying anything about the physical
world. Words and objects formed separate worlds. Novalis ignored
Tiedemann's censure of Plotinus because he believed in a Leibnizian
"preestablished harmony" between objects and concepts. As he
stated in his *Monolog*, precisely because language plays only with
itself it reflects "the strange interplay of objects" (II, 672). Thus,
he could conceive of a Plotinian "logical physics" (III, 179) and an
"experimental physics of the mind" (III, 595)—that is, of an "experimentation with images and concepts in the imagination" analogous to physical experimentation (III, 443). In part, this coincides
with what physicists today call "thought experiment"; though Novalis went a step further, believing that "the concepts of matter,
phlogiston, oxygen, gas, or force" were not signs for material objects
but creative symbols with which man could "boldly reach into universal chaos and forge his order from it" (III, 179). Hence science,
like art, was a constructive activity of intellect and imagination:
"Only when imaginative materials and forces are made into regu-
lative standards of natural materials and forces shall we become
physicists" (III, 448).

This statement is unrepresentative, though not unique (we shall
encounter a similar one referring to medicine): Novalis did place
theoretical and imaginative science above fact collection, but Werner taught him that science could not dispense with careful empirical
observations, which he saw as a necessary correlate to the imaginative construction of theories. In contrast to Schelling, who wanted
to construct science through deduction from a priori principles,
Novalis stressed imagination and experimentation. Being neither
an empiricist nor a rationalist, he favored imaginative hypotheses
and testing in the manner of the "hypothetico-deductive" model of
science:

Hypotheses are nets; only those will catch who cast them. Wasn't even
America found through a hypothesis? [. . .] The true hypothetician is but
an inventor to whom the discovered land often vaguely presents itself even
before the invention, he is someone who hovers with this vague image

above observation and experiment. Through a free comparison, through multiple encounters and frictions with experience he finally hits upon the [right] idea [. . .]. (II, 668f.)[9]

We shall encounter the same view in the novel fragment *Die Lehrlinge zu Sais*.

VI   *Brownian Medicine*

Novalis developed the physiological and medical counterpart to his logical physics while reading various German adaptions of the medical theory of the Scotch physician John Brown (1735–1788). Like the Plotinian physicist, Brown coerces nature:

The best part of Brown's system is the astonishing confidence with which Brown presents his system as universally valid. It should and must be so, experience and nature may say whatever they want. Therein lies the essence of every system, its truly effective force. Brown's system will thereby become the true system for his followers. Nothing can be said against this basically. The greater the magician, the more arbitrary his method, his utterances, his means. (II, 545f.)

Novalis later came to recognize that this was an extreme view, and he became critical of the dogmatism in Brownian medicine, adding to this criticism a second, diametrically opposed, target: while Brown was a forceful creative theorist, the principles underlying the doctrines of his *Elements of Medicine* were mechanistic and therefore incompatible with the notion of human freedom. According to the *Elements*, which significantly contributed to the emergence of *Naturphilosophie*, a quantity or excitability is assigned to each organism at the outset of life. This excitability is recharged during rest, but nevertheless slowly depleted by constant exposure to external excitation from the world of thinking and feeling. In a state of health, the rate of depletion is minimal, constant, and proportionate to the available amount of excitability, while excess or lack of excitation leads to sickness. Accordingly, only two types of diseases exist: sthenic diseases are caused by overstimulation, asthenic ones by understimulation. The art of healing aims at the restoration of a balance between stimulation and excitability.

Brown inherited from the eighteenth century the mechanistic

notion that life was sustained largely by impinging external stimuli. This was Novalis' prime target. His first reference to Brown is a marginal note to a generalization of Newton's second law—"every change has to have an external cause"—which consists of a question mark and the remark: "vid. Brown's system—contra Fichte" (II, 383), implying that Brown's system rested on mechanical principles which were opposed to Fichte's principle of active self-determination. Later notes confirm this: "all life is an uninterrupted stream" (II, 575); "life can only be explained by life" (III, 369); "the mistake of Brown's system is its leaning toward mechanism" (III, 407). This criticism was shared by other Romantics and Idealists, and so the German "improvements" over Brown consisted largely of attempts to reconcile his doctrines with a theory of self-sustaining life. Adalbert Röschlaub, the most important Brownian theoretician in Germany, distinguished, for instance, between an active and a receptive component of excitability, to enable the body to play a more active role in the maintenance of health and life. However, Röschlaub's continued adherence to mechanistic principles challenged Novalis to formulate a critique; though he apparently never worked it out, relevant remarks are scattered throughout his notebooks. Novalis was fascinated by the attempt to formulate a philosophical approach to the art of healing; he found the systems of Brown and his followers wanting, but considered them as a first step from empiricism toward a science of general principles.

VII   *Magic Idealism*

The theory of Magic Idealism grows out, in part, of Novalis' studies in medicine and physiology and culminates in a series of notes which were probably written at the beginning of the year 1798 (II, 545ff.). Essentially, Novalis envisages a lengthy training to gradually reduce our dependence on sensory stimulation and to replace external physical impulses by psychic ones. In the final stage, the senses would no longer be mere receptors of the sights and sounds of the world, but active organs directed by psychic energies and giving palpable expression to mental states in the form of hallucinations and visions. The body would thus become a shaping and creating tool. The potential for creatively redefining the self is, according to Novalis, dormant in all men; the artist is merely further advanced in developing his skill to manipulate matter by shaping stone, mixing colors, or combining sounds (II, 574 and 584). In general, magic is "the art of arbitrarily using the physical world" (II, 546). If Plotinian mysticism regards the physical world as an overflow of God's energy, Magic Idealism asserts that art is an emanation of the human spirit.

Here we run into some problems. The "arbitrary" use of the senses and objects seems to amount to a dominance and exploitation of nature which Novalis criticized in Fichte. How could nature be a "thou" if it is to be treated arbitrarily? No categorical answer can be given to this question, for at least in one passage, Novalis himself saw Magic Idealism as a step beyond Fichte (II, 605). On the basis of such passages, Hermann August Korff and others have arrived at a "Fichtean" interpretation of Magic Idealism and of Novalis' thought in general: [Magic Idealism] "draws from the fundamental idea of subjectivism—the creative freedom of the subject—the most extreme conclusion and turns the subject theoretically and practically into a miracle worker, magician, and a sorcerer; indeed he must become this if the empirical self gradually assumes the capabilities of the absolute."[10] This view is too simple, but unfortunately we have space only for two major comments. First, Magic Idealism represents merely a stage in Novalis' development; it does not occur in the later notebooks and appears merely as one of many possible views in the fictional works. Novalis' turn to literature and his concomitant preparation for a modest domestic life may, in themselves, be seen as signs that he scaled down his expectations and came to see magic as restricted to linguistic-poetic transformations only. Second, even some of the central passages on Magic Idealism indicate that he did not envisage a total subordination of the senses to the creative power of the mind:

I would find my sense or body determined partly by itself, partly through the idea of the whole, through its spirit, the world-soul. The two would be so inextricably united that one couldn't assert one or the other exclusively. [. . .] I find my body determined and active by itself and by the world-soul. My body is a small whole and has therefore also a specific soul—for I call soul that through which everything becomes one whole, the individualizing principle. (II, 551)

This suggests that body and matter were for Novalis no mere not I, but part of a cosmos animated by a world soul. The ego that manipulates the world is in some "preestablished harmony" with matter and its animating soul, and hence the magic manipulation of nature is based on an underlying harmony and agreement with her.

VIII *Romantization*

Magic Idealism actually implies simultaneous overcoming of the world and the self, as Novalis formulated it in one of his most famous fragments. "Romantization" is not an indulgence in sentimentality, but a process metaphorically repesented by raising the self to a higher power in a geometric series:

The world must be romanticized. Thus will its original meaning be rediscovered. Romanticizing is nothing but a qualitative raise to a higher power. The lower self will be identified in this operation with a better self. Just as we ourselves are such a qualitative series of raises to higher powers. This operation is still quite unknown. When I endow the vulgar with a noble meaning, the common with a mysterious appearance, the known with the dignity of the unknown, the finite with the semblance of infinitude, I romanticize. The operation for the higher, unknown, mystic, and infinite is the reverse—its logarithm will be taken in this mode of combination and it will thereby acquire a familiar expression. Romantic philosophy. Lingua romana. Reciprocal heightening and lowering. (II, 545)

Two processes are actually telescoped in this fragment: raising to a higher power and romantization. Both are activities of the self, but raising to a higher power is inner-directed, while romantization is a way of perceiving the world. The first, which is the precondition of the second, utilizes the Fichtean distinction between the lower and the higher self in terms of a mathematical metaphor: the purification of the self is a "qualitative" po er series in which the empirical self raises itself to ever higher levels of consciousness toward the infinitely removed pure self. Intensified consciousness allows the romantization of the world—a creative remaking of it not through technological manipulation but through a mode already suggested in *Blütenstaub:* the philistine and prosaic perception of the world must give way to a marvel and wonder at its mysterious magnificence. As a correlate, we ought to infuse everyday life with our sense of the distant, strange, and higher. Romantization is a heightening of the physical world, for instance, through an erotic mystification of the flesh, and a perception of palpable reality as a symbolic revelation of a spiritual and moral order. The very wording indicates that this is an attempt to reawaken the slumbering religious sense primarily through the means of poetry and art, the special, though paradigmatic, modes of romantization. Because of this link between religion, poetry, and reality, compared to the plan of the *Lyrical Ballads* (conceived of almost exactly at the same time by Coleridge and Wordsworth) as recounted in Coleridge's *Biographia Literaria:*

it was agreed that my endeavours should be directed to persons and characters supernatural, or at least romantic; yet so as to transfer from our inward nature a human interest and a semblance of truth sufficient to procure for these shadows of imagination that willing suspension of disbelief for the moment, which constitutes poetic faith. Mr. Wordsworth, on the other hand, was to propose to himself as his object to give the charm of novelty to things of every day, and to excite a feeling analogous to the supernatural, by awakening the mind's attention from the lethargy of custom and directing it to the loveliness and the wonders of the world before us; an inexhaustible treasure, but for which, in consequence of the film of familiarity and selfish solicitude, we have eyes yet see not, ears that hear not, and hearts that neither feel nor understand.[11]

Thus, in Novalis' terminology, Coleridge took upon himself the "logarithmification" of the supernatural and Wordsworth the "heightening" of the ordinary. The parallel is striking, though it would not be profitable to insist on correspondences in detail. Coleridge's "Kubla Khan" or Wordsworth's "Tintern Abbey" have much in common with Novalis' *Hymmen an die Nacht* and his other poems, but they are written in a different idiom and seem to distinguish between poetic and religious faith, or between truth and poetic truth, in a way that Novalis would not have approved of. Nevertheless, it is fascinating to contemplate that the best poets of German and English Romanticism had similar ideas even though they knew nothing of each other.

CHAPTER 4

Apprenticeship in Literature:
Die Lehrlinge zu Sais

FEW works are comparable in originality and amplitude of conception to the incomplete *Die Lehrlinge*. Begun amidst the scientific studies of Freiberg and shelved when Novalis later turned to other projects, *Die Lehrlinge* attempts to accommodate an encyclopedic range of scientific and philosophic thought in a *Bildungsroman*, a novel of education. The saturation of the text with philosophy and science anticipates the encyclopedic modern novels, while its abstraction and lyrical texture prepare the ground for the fictional mode of Maurice Maeterlinck, André Gide, Virginia Woolf, or Hermann Hesse.[1] Readers coming to the text with expectations nourished by the narrative novel will be disappointed: the fragment has no setting and no characterization in the usual sense; the "plot" consists of inner monologues and conversations between disembodied voices that are difficult to identify. The sights and sounds of the world become verbal signs in the void of interior space into which "everything leads back" (I, 81). Since the conversational subjects are mostly scientific and philosophical, one may characterize *Die Lehrlinge* as a lyrical treatise on man's relationship to nature and himself.

Lucretius' *The Way Things Are*, perhaps the most successful philosophic-scientific poem ever written, shows that lyrical tone and philosophic subject are not incompatible, difficult though they may be to harmonize. Unfortunately, the incompleteness and shifting point of view of *Die Lehrlinge* makes comprehension so difficult that critics widely disagree on its meaning and achievement.[2] In my view, *Die Lehrlinge* offers no consistent *Naturphilosophie*, although it may be moving toward one. Since aesthetic and conceptual variety are more characteristic for it than unity, the work may best be

64

appreciated as an exploration of various natural philosophies in a correspondingly rich variety of rhetorical forms.

The knowledge of self and nature and the relationship between them form the thematic center of the text. *Die Lehrlinge* essentially represents a lyrical confrontation between the philosophical and scientific ideas that concerned Novalis during 1797 and 1798. Since the narrator-novice, whose views are probably closest to Novalis' own, speaks only briefly toward the end of the first chapter, and the remaining views are mostly foils against which presumably a final synthesis would have been formulated, there is no real resolution to the questions raised; but the poetic language and the coupling of self-knowledge with knowledge of nature implies answers opposed to the notion of an "objective" science and the separation of "facts" from "value."

I *Genesis*

In a letter of February 24, 1798, Novalis mentioned to August Wilhelm Schlegel that he was working on a fragment project called "The Novice of Sais," probably the draft of the first chapter now called "The Novice." Sporadic notebook entries show that he continued to work on it in Freiberg; he abandoned it when, upon returning to Weißenfels, he became preoccupied with professional and domestic plans and changed his ideas on art as a result of his friendship with Tieck. On February 23, 1800, Novalis thanked Tieck for calling to his attention the mystic thought of Jakob Boehme and added: "So much the better that *Die Lehrlinge*, which should appear now in a completely different light, is resting. It should become a truly symbolic *(sinnbldlich)* novel of nature. *Heinrich von Ofterdingen* must be finished first." Since Novalis made no further changes in *Die Lehrlinge* after this letter, his new perspective, which would have shifted the novel toward a Boehmean mystic-symbolic view of nature, did not materialize. We are thus dealing with a fragment that Novalis considered unsatisfactory.

The title neatly indicates that Novalis' project was stimulated by two literary models, Goethe's *Wilhelm Meisters Lehrjahre* and Schiller's poem "Das verschleierte Bild zu Sais" ("The Veiled Image at Sais"). *Wilhelm Meister* was a *Bildungsroman*, a novel of education, and Novalis adopted this novelistic genre both in *Die Lehrlinge* and in *Ofterdingen*, in spite of his inreasing dissatisfaction

with Goethe's use of it. He was to expose his novices to years of
apprenticeship, though he may have planned different experiences
for them. Apprenticeship is the subject also of Goethe's ballad "Der
Zauberlehrling" ("The Sorcerer's Apprentice," 1798), which may
have been on Novalis' mind while writing the tale of "Hyazinth and
Rosenblütchen" for the second chapter of *Die Lehrlinge*. Goethe's
apprentice exploits his master's absence to conjure up demonic
powers with magic formulas, but is unable to keep them under
control because he doesn't understand the meaning of the formulas.
Novalis' Hyazinth makes a similar mistake by following the letter
of his mentor's book, but finally goes out into the world to learn by
experience.

The choice of a setting in the Egyptian temple of Sais indicates
Novalis' debt to Schiller's poem. Schiller's novice is so possessed
by a desire to know "the whole truth" that he lifts the veil of the
goddess against her express injunction. We never learn what he
sees, but are warned not to follow his example. Thus Schiller treats
in a dramatic key the comic theme of Goethe's ballad: both describe
acts of transgression in search of truth and power, respectively, to
illustrate the need for self-constraint. Novalis used Goethe's and
Schiller's theme to negate the injunction against transgression. His
novice's free quest for knowledge is sanctioned by the conviction
that if mortals are forbidden to lift the veil of the goddess, "we must
seek to become immortal; he who does not seek to lift it is no
genuine novice at Sais" (I, 82). Knowledge of the world therefore
becomes a function of personal growth. In May 1798, Novalis wrote
a distich, where the lifted veil reveals the self (I, 110), and a poem
"Kenne dich selbst" ("Know Thyself"), where the quest for knowledge yields self-knowledge:[3]

Glücklich, wer weise geworden und nicht die Welt mehr durchgrübelt,
Wer von sich selber den Stein ewiger Weisheit begehrt.
Nur der vernünftige Mensch ist der ächte Adept—er verwandelt
Alles in Leben und Gold—braucht Elixire nicht mehr.
In ihm dampfet der heilige Kolben—der König ist in ihm—
Delphos auch und er faßt endlich das: *Kenne dich selbst*. (I, 404)

(Lucky are those who have become wise and no longer worry about the
world, / those who are desirous of the stone of wisdom in themselves. /
Only reasonable men are true adepts—they transform / everything into life

and gold—need elixirs no longer. / In them the holy retort is steaming—
kings reside in them— / Delphi too and they finally grasp the *Know Thyself.*)

II   *Chapter I: The Novice*

The first of the two chapters amounts to merely eight paragraphs;
its "plot" consists of a series of shifts in the narrative voice. The
title suggests that the narrator is a novice at the temple, but the
text reveals him only gradually. The first paragraph is impersonal,
the second and third identify an "I" in passing but immediately shift
to another speaker, the long fourth one finally introduces a person
as "our teacher," creating thereby a community of teacher and
novices. The last three paragraphs contain the novice's personal
statement. If we can thus observe the emergence of a personality,
nothing gets spatially defined or described. The visible world is
indicated merely by the use of a few standard adjectives and by a
long, unconnected catalogue of objects in the opening sentences:

Man pursues manifold paths. Whoever traces and compares them will see
strange figures emerge, figures which seem to belong to that great cipher-
writing which one perceives everywhere: on wings and eggshells, in clouds,
snow, crystals, and rock formations, on freezing water, in the interior and
exterior of mountains, plants, animals, and men, in the lights of the sky,
on touched and rubbed discs of pitch and glass, in the iron filings around
a magnet, and in the strange conjunctures of chance. (I, 79)

The remarkable verbal virtuosity of this passage reveals something
about the intent of the novel. The phenomena of the visible world,
which include the common sights of nature as well as the secrets
she divulges in experimentally contrived situations, are—but mere
ciphers of secret forms described by nature and the divergent paths
of man: the ways of man and nature are identical; self-knowledge
and understanding of nature are two forms of the same statement.

But according to the following sentences, the letters of nature's
script yield no message, moments of divination are swallowed by
oblivion. This complaint is countered in the short second and third
paragraphs by the reply that the meaning of nature cannot be crys-
talized into conceptual language because she speaks unconsciously,

her "holy scripture" being a musical sound, "a chord from the symphony of the universe." Indeed, all genuine languages are intentionless, speak "because speaking is their pleasure and essence"; nature's language is like the language of poetry and mathematics which Novalis characterized in his *Monolog*.

But how can one understand nature's language and be a novice to its wisdom if there is no clear meaning to it? This question is answered by way of typical indirection in the fourth and fifth paragraphs, when the teacher recounts that he had learned it by careful observation and collection of natural objects, by an analysis of his impressions of them, and by gradually recognizing a network of similarities and affinities among them. But since, like nature itself, he is mute about his final insight and his way of finding it, those novices who expect a formal instruction by rules return home and take up another profession—though the teacher insists that by finding their own way they will know what happened to him. Among those he sends out to find their way and to return one day are two symbolic figures, a child, suggestive of Christ, and a clumsy youngster. To the former he wanted to entrust teaching immediately after his arrival, and he now predicts that the lessons will come to an end upon his return. The clumsy youngster was sent with the child because, though he was no good in methodical observations, he accidentally found the stone that was needed to fill the central spot of the mineral collection.

Both the child and the youngster are exemplary novices, then, in that they rely on their intuition instead of on doctrinal teaching. Their characterization prepares for the self-portrayal of the speaker-novice in the last three paragraphs of the chapter: he feels affinity with the child-novice, he is clumsier than others, and he gains the teacher's confidence by not following him. Although he enjoys the sight of objects, he seeks the reflection of divine light in them. He hesitates between wanting to travel in distant strange lands and staying in the temple, but whatever the "figure" of his life is going to be, his path will have to lead back to his home at the holy place.

The surrealistic interchange of voices thus intimates ties between knowledge, nature, and self-development. Instead of a sequence of events, we get hints about the future and recollections about the teacher's past which enlarge the temporal scope of the situation and suggest patterns of development. Such a development is the subject of the fairy tale insert of Chapter Two.

III   *The Tale of Hyazinth and Rosenblütchen*

Hyazinth, the "novice" of the tale, is a young lad estranged from his family and his sweetheart, Rosenblütchen, walking around in a state of aberration, talking incomprehensibly to birds, trees, and rocks, but deaf to their attempts to lighten his seriousness with poetic entertainment. He changed from a cheerful state to melancholy during the visit of an old man, a teacher figure, who returned Hyazinth's hospitality by telling him stories about wonderful distant lands and customs. Rosenblütchen considers the old man a sorcerer (reference to Goethe's poem?) because he left behind an undecipherable book which apparently caused Hyazinth's derangement. One day Hyazinth meets a strange old woman who burns the book and suggests that he should leave home to find a cure. Hyazinth is driven into the world by a vague but powerful urge to find the "mother of things," the veiled virgin. In the course of a long, erratic, and yet mysteriously purposeful journey, his mind slowly mellows, his restlessness settles, and he is able to reestablish communication with the world. In this state of attunement with nature, he finally encounters the goddess in a dream, "for only dream could lead him into the holiest realm," and discovers behind the lifted veil, Rosenblütchen.

Such plot outline can merely indicate the tale's contour of meaning, but cannot do justice to its artful simplicity. The simplicity is evident in the choice of words, in the clear syntax, and in the sustained light tone, the artfulness in the camouflaged complex compositional and philosophical principles. While an earlier sketch (I, 110) contains a simple, linear narrative, the final version recounts the state of harmony preceding the derangement as a flashback and develops a more complex and differentiated narrative. Nevertheless, Novalis retains his triadic concept of history: the initial state of naive harmony is interrupted by a fall and a period of unrest, but harmony is finally restored on a higher level. The fallen state, which is the subject of the narrative, may be subdivided further into several states of mind and relationships to nature.

The fall from idyllic happiness is due to a desire for the fruits of knowledge, aroused in Hyazinth by the encounter with the old man and his book. But, as elsewhere in Novalis' writing, the fall is necessary to reach a higher level of existence. Hyazinth's alienation from Rosenblütchen, his family, and nature is not due to any Mephistophelian seduction, but rather to his mistaken effort to emulate his mentor by using his book. As the first chapter states in the spirit of Fichte's teaching, education cannot be codified and reduced to a book. The mentor's true legacy is therefore not the book but the message that Hyazinth should go out into the world and find his own way. Until the burning of the book, Hyazinth's course of action was erroneous. During the journey, he learns to see the way things are and to control his yearning for the unknown. Since exploration of the self and of the world are two sides of the same coin, predictably, Hyazinth discovers in the distance his rejuvenated self and domestic happiness with his childhood sweetheart. Rosenblütchen's love apparently hinders the physical and spiritual journey, but actually serves as its guiding spirit under the veil of the goddess. Thus Hyazinth's love for Rosenblütchen is the earthly aspect of that divine love which appears in the first chapter as a yearning for the goddess. The same dual love reappears later in the *Hymnen an die Nacht*, directed toward the beloved and the heavenly mother; it was a recurrent subject of Novalis' correspondence at the time when he tried to reconcile his new found love for Julie with the commitment to the transfigured Sophie.

IV   Chapter II: Nature

The tale of Hyazinth and Rosenblütchen appears toward the middle of the fragmentary second chapter. It is preceded by an opening reflective passage, presumably narrated by the novice, and a discussion between unidentified speakers which is so confusing that only the narration of the tale by a "cheerful playmate" can straighten out the novice. At the end of the narration, the novices embrace each other and depart; after brief comments by the "spirits of the place," newly arrived travelers engage in a discussion which comes to an abrupt end with the reappearance of the teacher.

The second chapter is longer than the first and attempts to capture a broader range of views, attitudes, and moods. It opens with a contrast between the unity of primitive man and the fragmentation in modern life, a topic which Novalis may have adopted from Schiller's aesthetic writings. Modern man's inability to reestablish a simple natural state by recombining the "dispersed colors of his spirit" or by establishing new combinations among them, is perhaps due to his "sickly disposition" (I, 82f). The consideration of the state of primitive man leads, in a loose and associative manner, to cosmo-logical theories. The speaker is fascinated primarily by the earliest poetic explanations of nature, where men, gods, and animals act as joint masterbuilders of the world. History of the world as human history and accidents of nature as acts of human personality were primitive conceptions that retained popularity because they sug-gested a unity between man and nature. Is the "poetic" approach to nature superior, then, to the scientific? The discussion drifts toward a qualification and final negation of the first suggestion that poets and naturalists originally spoke the same language and were therefore part of the same community (I, 84). While poets provide daily delight to the heart with their concrete approach to nature, scientists seek to ascertain her universal rules with sharp dissecting knives, exploring the inner structure and relationship of her mem-bers. Thus nature leaves only "dead twitching remainders" (an im-age taken from galvanic experiments with frog legs) in the hands of the scientists while it celebrates dionysian rites with the poet. It must therefore be concluded: "Those who truly want to know [nature's] spirit must seek her in the company of poets; there she is open and pours her wonderful heart out. But those who do not love her from the bottom of their heart, and who admire or wish to learn merely this and that about her, must diligently visit her at the sickbed or in the charnel-house" (I, 84).

This ironic contrast concludes the historical considerations and leads to a rephrasing of the novel's opening sentence: the ways of nature and man are equally varied, "to say there is only one nature is to exaggerate" (I, 85). The attitudes toward nature are now grouped under the aspect of time: some people seek in nature their past, a lost home, "a beloved of their youth, parents or sisters and brothers, old friends, fond memories," whereas others expect to find beyond nature the lively world of the future. "Few pause calmly amidst these magnificent surroundings," merely to grasp their rich-ness and interconnections. "Thus are born the different ways of contemplating nature, and if, at one extreme, the sentiment of nature becomes an amusing fancy, a meal, elsewhere one sees it transformed into a most pious religion, giving direction, support, and meaning to a whole life" (I, 85).

At this point, the essayistic form can no longer encompass the multiple perspective, and the single voice is replaced by six speakers and points of views, of which only the last two, "a serious man" and

a "cheerful playmate" (the narrator of Hyazinth's tale), are identified. They do not seem to fit into an evolutionary sequence, but
they may be divided into two groups: those who seek a friendly
union with nature (the first speaker and the playmate) and those
who see the confrontation between nature and reason inevitable
(the four middle speakers). Only the second speaker answers directly, while the other views are presented as independent statements rather than parts of a dialogue: the speakers enounce rather
than respond. This may be taken as a sign of arrogance, but also as
an admission that the plurality of approaches to nature is a necessity.
The intellectual confusion arising from the conflicting theories can
therefore be resolved only by the tale, which is introduced by the
following address to the novice: "You brooder, you follow the wrong
path, and this way you will not make much progress. Mood is what
counts" (I, 91). Accordingly, the style of the tale creates a mood
from which the message is inseparable. The six speakers cannot be
identified unequivocally, though they do represent philosophical
attitudes that Novalis encountered in his readings and personal
contacts. Their views and styles are actually often inconsistent. The
first and most elaborate statement, for instance, calls for an ennoblement and humanization of nature's great but uncultivated gardens through ceaseless toil. During the enumeration of the various
activities to domesticate and soften the savage nature, the speaker
switches from the narrative past to the present and then to a utopian
future, envisioned in a series of "then" clauses. But the vision of
a new golden age is abruptly terminated and followed by sober
advices that counter the earlier ones. If the humanization of nature
required that man impose his image upon her, now empiricism, a
childlike surrender to nature, is recommended, and the future philosopher is recognized "in those who ceaselessly investigate and
question all natural things" (I, 87).

To this, "some" respond that the careful observation of nature is
not only wasteful but dangerous. Nature is a "devouring monster"
intent on destroying man: "Association with natural forces, with
animals, plants, rocks, storms, and waves will necessarily assimilate
man to these; and the assimilation, transformation, and dissolution
of what is divine and human into uncontrolled forces is the spirit
of this dreaded devouring power called nature" (I, 89). Bolder voices
echo Schiller's urging that the liberating war against nature be carried out jointly by poets and scientists, and their call is followed by

more contemplative voices: "Why should we wearily journey through the gloomy world of visible things? The purer world lies within us, in this well-head" (I, 89). Finally a "serious man" adopts a highly moralistic attitude based on the principles of Fichte: "The others talk nonsense. [. . .] Don't they recognize in nature the true imprint of their self? [. . .] The meaning of the world is reason. [. . .] Whoever should wish to gain a knowledge of nature must exercise his moral sense, must act and mold according to the noble center of his inner self, and nature will reveal herself to him, as if by her own will" (I, 90).

The tale of the "cheerful playmate," and not the high-minded moral principles of the last speaker, provide the resolution which presumably foreshadows the future harmonization of conflict in the temple of Sais. After the tale, the novices depart with a symbolic embrace, but the "voices of the objects in the sacred halls," the "spirits of the place," lament their separation from man and thereby accentuate the contrast between the fictional and the fairytale worlds. The objects yearn for the primitive harmony in which man was dominated by feeling, and cannot believe that his reason and his aspiration to become God will achieve a reunification: "Thought is but a dream of feeling, a withered feeling, a pale-grey feeble life" (I, 96).

The discussion of the remainder of the chapter is carried out between four travelers who come to stay overnight. They do not respond to each other genuinely, but their two rounds of statements allow the reader to identify the positions more clearly.[4] The roles are uneven: the second traveler hardly speaks, while the fourth, the only one given an identification, makes an elaborate closing statement. Being a "beautiful youth," his poetic view of nature is comparable to the "cheerful playmate's."

The first traveler envisions a play with perceptions, familiar to us from Novalis' "Magic Idealism." The deliberate shifts of attention, the arbitrary registration, magnification, reduction, or elimination of perceptions constitute a game, which is a magnificent manifestation of man's freedom and superiority to nature. Yet we do not know whether external nature can be understood through our body, which is a part of her. In order to find out, we must observe carefully the thought processes relating to each perception and learn to recall sensations at will: "Once we have mastered a few of these thought processes as the alphabet of nature, the decoding would become ever simpler, and our power over the generation and flow of thoughts would enable us as observers to create a nature of ideas and to design compositions of nature without preceding sensations; and then the final goal would be attained" (I, 98). The theory appears in the second round of statements as a modification of Fichte's theory. The playful use of sensations must not be understood as an elimination of nature; nature is "a means and a medium of an agreement between intelligent beings." In creatively contemplating nature, man returns to his original mode of being "where creating and knowing existed in wondrous reciprocity." If he surrenders to the vision (Novalis uses the term *Beschauung*—a characteristic shift from Fichtean cogitation!) of the primordial intellectual intuition, nature's genesis unfolds before his eyes, forming a bond between himself and nature's self: "The careful description of this inner world history is the true theory of nature; the inner coherence of his idea cosmos and its harmony with the universe will spontaneously yield a system of thought that is a faithful image and formula of the universe" (I, 101).

Thus, the first speaker stresses the "preestablished harmony" between human "compositions of nature" and the nature of the universe, in the manner of Novalis' *Monolog*. To this, the second speaker replies that we cannot construct a unified picture of nature from our haphazardly received perceptions. It would be more reasonable to see nature as a "product of an incomprehensible consensus of infinitely diverse beings" (I, 98). While the first speaker eventually convinces the second to abandon this view, the third speaker actually radicalizes the position by praising hypotheses in the manner of Novalis' fifth dialogue: "the more haphazardly the bold fisherman's net is woven, the luckier the catch. Let us encourage everybody to go furthest his way and welcome everybody who enmeshes *(überspinnt)* the objects with fresh imagination" (I, 98). If the scientist-thinker works like an artist and moves with his mind in such a way that the universe is reduced to a figure of mysterious appearance (an obvious reference to Newton), he "dances nature," verbally traces the lines of her motions, so that here too creation and observation merge (I, 102). This speaker nevertheless knows that creative knowledge is limited, first because such designs cannot recount nature's history: those who play with nature as if fantasizing on a great instrument achieve no genuine insight, for this is "the gift of the historian of nature, the seer of time. [. . .] Everything divine has a history" (I, 99). Second, the creative approach to nature must be complemented by careful observations and childlike receptivity to nature's divine messages:

> There are other friends of knowledge besides the thinker who are not eminently devoted to creation through thinking; instead of regarding this art as a calling, they rather become students of nature who find their joy in learning rather than in teaching, in experience rather than in making, in receiving rather than in giving. [. . .] The idlest ones among them expect like a child to receive the knowledge of nature that is useful to them through loving communications from higher beings they fervently adore. They do not wish to spend time and pay attention in this short life to business that would divert them from the service of love. (I, 102f)

The "beautiful youth," finally, praises the poets, for "only poets have felt what nature can be to man" (I, 99) and conceived her as living totality rather than an accumulation of mindless mechanical parts. Contrary to the usual view, poets do not exaggerate enough, they are unaware of the orphic powers slumbering in their voices: "Doesn't the rock become a unique Thou if I address it?" (I, 100). Inverting the notion that "beauty vivifies," the youth suggests that the sublime petrifies; minerals and rocks might thus have become petrified at the sight of a divinity. The second speech of the youth opens with the portrayal of man's loving surrender to the contrasting primordial forces of fluid and flame: "What is the flame that is visible everywhere? An intimate embrace whose sweet fruit condenses in arduous drops. Water, this first-born child of airy unions, cannot deny its sensuous origin and reveals itself as the element of love and as the admixture of earth with divine omnipotence" (I, 104). In the following long praise of fluidity, the "mother of all things," the sober scientific approach to nature is shown to be inferior to mystic and pantheistic submissions to her embrace. The true lover of nature will enjoy her as a bride: "I praise as happy this son, this darling of nature, whom she allows to contemplate her as a duality, as a power that engenders and bears, and as unity, as an endless and everlasting marriage. His life is going to be a plenitude of all pleasures, a chain of voluptuousness; his religion the actual true naturalism" (I, 106).

These words end the youth's second speech and the discussion of the travelers. The teacher and the novices return now, and the travelers reveal themselves as seekers of a lost primeval language which, so the legend says, once possessed the magic of reaching all powers of the universe and unlocking the secret of objects. The teacher refers them to a future language of higher synthesis: the true prophet of nature must speak of her with "worship and faith" and "devise a system based on experiment, analysis, and comparison."

At this point, the text breaks off abruptly, leaving the reader at a stage that corresponds to Hyazinth's state of confusion before his journey. Presumably, the novel would have continued with the novice's apprenticeship-journey, but we don't even have sketches to help us imagine how Novalis would have worked this out.

The multiple perspective of *Die Lehrlinge* may perhaps be best appreciated as a bold intellectual and artistic experiment. Innovative above all is the way in which Novalis fused the three genre-modes to create a fictional text consisting of dramatic monologues and dialogues written in a lyrical and rhapsodic style. The formal experiment deeply affects the philosophic and scientific content: the attempted "poetization" of knowledge is a deliberate move beyond the fragment and the discursive essay, in search of an encyclopedic synthesis of man and nature. Though the experiment remains incomplete and could not have succeeded, the attempt itself is admirable. Carlyle, with characteristic caution, described it as a very mysterious fragment, "disclosing scientific depth, which we have not light to see into, much less means to fathom and accurately measure," while Maurice Maeterlinck thought that "there are few works more mysterious, more serene, and more beautiful" and prepared a French translation of it.[5]

CHAPTER 5

The Theorist of State, Religion, and History

I   Political Involvement

BECAUSE of the incomplete victory of absolutism, Saxony's eighteenth-century legal and political system retained feudal vestiges amidst enlightened rationalism. Residential (*amtsässige*) landowners, such as the Hardenbergs, were automatically members of the upper house in the *Landtag* with a vote, and they were also charged with the judicial and police organization of their district. Novalis' father entered state service because of his precarious financial situation, but he was proud of the traditional privileges and freedom of his class, which stood in conflict with the absolutist aspirations and reforms of the king. Novalis retained some aspects of this feudal notion of freedom.

Young Novalis had actually little interest in Saxon politics, for his allegiance belonged to the Reich. He wrote laudatory verses for Frederick the Great as well as for Joseph II because for him this was a formal exercise and not a commitment to their state or their ideals. He felt that the selfish particularism of the states had destroyed that Reich from which he could expect the emergence of that supranational and confessional Europe in which he ultimately believed. Yet he was unwilling to enter the political arena to fight for his ideal because he was disinterested in the power play between states or in courtly and parliamentary intrigue; ideal politics were to him no politics at all.[1]

The wave of revolutionary enthusiasm which carried the young Hegel, Hölderlin, Schiller, and many others apparently left Novalis unruffled while in Jena, although he was later to report that the democratic fashion of those days had turned him "disloyal to the old aristocratic faith" (IV, 310). Under the influence of Friedrich Schlegel, he became more receptive to revolutionary ideas in Leipzig; there and in Wittenberg, he socialized with a group of noblemen around Hans Georg Carlowitz which became active in Saxon politics during the following years, trying to steer a middle of the road liberalism between conservatism and, as Carlowitz put it, the "sansculottism of our knighted despots" (IV, 521). In 1799, Carlowitz wanted Novalis to take a look at the "ridiculous parliamentary circus" in Dresden and to join the "third party." Novalis' reply, though lost, may be reconstituted from Carlowitz' next letter and a note in the "Brouillon" (III, 474). Precisely because he shared Carlowitz' contempt for the political circus, Novalis had no desire to participate in the Saxon diet. The nobility's liberal opposition to centralized cameralistic and mercantilistic power seemed to him not much more worthy of support than the conservative cause, and he saw a genuine possibility that the traditional privileges of the Saxon nobility would soon be abolished. On the other hand, he had no special loyalty to the Saxon state, even though he came to serve it in a technical and bureaucratic capacity; occasionally, for instance during the debate about Fichte's alleged atheism, he was critical of its suppression of personal freedom. Carlowitz regretted Novalis' decision, for only he "could elevate a whole generation and suppress the hated voice of selfishness, stupidity, and brutality" (IV, 520). Several years later, Carlowitz and his friends did help in carrying out reforms in Saxony.

Novalis stayed away from politics and never developed a program of political action that could have turned the existing institutions into the ideal state he envisioned. He accepted the French Revolution as a historical necessity, but the political structures that emerged from it were not congenial to his thinking. Seeing that neither the revolution nor the traditional political system could appropriately alter the state of affairs, he came to espouse a credo of personal development whose revolutionary long-range effect allowed a temporary accommodation within the existing social and political institutions, even a sincere service of the state: "Since personal education was perceived as a human mission, this limitation to the private sphere could be well reconciled with a revolutionary disposition and an inner rebellion against the ruling powers."[2]

Novalis' accommodation was furthered by his lack of patriotism.

As a letter to his mother from June 1793 indicates, his primary attachment belonged to the family: "The family is still closer to me than the state. [. . .] One is a perfect citizen of the state when one exists first and foremost for one's family. The well-being of the state consists of the well-being of the individual families. Only through my family am I immediately tied to my country—which could otherwise be as indifferent to me as any other state" (IV, 121). Novalis essentially held on to this view; it allowed him to identify in *Glauben und Liebe* the state as a symbolic family, while in the "Brouillon" he was to remark: "The state doesn't consist of individuals, but of couples and societies" (III, 470).

Due to this indifference toward state affairs, he could not readily put his law degree to use. In May 1794, Novalis asked his father to help him find a position to gain financial independence, and added: "I completely leave to you the choice of means and remind you merely that Saxony doesn't offer the most advantageous prospects. [. . .] *Ubi bene, ibi patria* (my country is where I like it)" (IV, 136). A letter to Friedrich Schlegel, written shortly before Novalis assumed his first job, indicates that pursuit of personal happiness and abstract political radicalism were at the time his foremost ethical concerns:

My whole character has received now almost imperceptibly a politico-philosophical impetus. [. . .] Things happen today which ten years ago were relegated to the madhouse of philosophy. [. . .] Every unusual man interests me now tenfold, because ere the age of equality arrives we shall need supernatural power. [. . .] These are the days of betrothal—still free and unattached and yet already committed by free choice—I impatiently long for wedding night, marriage, and offspring. If heaven should turn my wedding night into a St. Bartholomew's night for despotism and jails, I'd celebrate happy days of marriage. My heart is heavy that the chains are not yet falling like the walls of Jericho. (IV, 140f.)

This unusual Jacobin tone weakened once Novalis took up his first job, but traces of his sympathy with the revolution may be found in his later life as well. In Tennstedt he missed the *Moniteur*, the official voice of the French Revolution (IV, 145), and according to Just, he was sufficiently impressed by the radical consistency of the Jacobins to deliver a panegyric on Robespierre's reign of terror (IV, 540f.). In the spring of 1797, he still sympathized with the composer and editor Johann Friedrich Reichardt, one of the most consistent supporters of the French Revolution. The diary of that summer notes: "Republicanism is awakened in me once more quite lively" (IV, 45)

II   Glauben und Liebe

The "engagement" foreseen in the quoted letter soon became a reality, but the personal as well as historical "wedding night" remained a dream. Three years later, Novalis expressed his political ideas in a fragment collection that celebrated the accession of Frederick Wilhelm III and his attractive wife Louise to the Prussian throne on November 16, 1797. *Glauben und Liebe* marks a new political position, but its novelty should not be overestimated: as the 1794 letter to Schlegel represented only one aspect of his views, so the defense of monarchy in *Glauben und Liebe* has to be reconciled with the surviving elements of republicanism in the collection.

The accession of Frederick Wilhelm III had already occasioned the longer fragment no. 122 in "Vermischte Bemerkungen" which was not included in *Blütenstaub*. Most fragments in *Glauben und Liebe* were probably written during the spring of 1798; Novalis read from them to August Wilhelm Schlegel at the end of March, and he sent off the manuscript to Friedrich on May 11, 1798, with the comment that it could not be read without "faith and love" (IV, 253). Schlegel placed the manuscript with the journal *Jahrbücher der preußischen Monarchie*, and the introductory poems, entitled "Blumen" ("Flowers"), promptly appeared in the June issue, followed in July by the fragments under the full title *Glauben und Liebe oder der König und die Königin (Faith and Love or the King and the Queen)*. The publication created a great sensation in Berlin (IV, 621), but the publisher soon had to report that due to the king's displeasure, the censors forbade the publication of the third installment (IV, 499), which was published under the title "Politische Aphorismen" only in the 1846 Novalis edition.

Unfortunately, only second and thirdhand information survives on the royal reaction. According to one source, the king found Novalis' remarks on the queen "tasteless and immoral" (IV, 622); another one quoted him as saying: "more is asked of a king than what he is capable of doing. People forget that he is a human being.

Let the men who remind the king of his duties be brought from their desk to the throne, then only will they see the surrounding difficulties that are impossible to surmount" (IV, 497). Schlegel commented that the king's serious response showed that "the literary and intellectual mediocrity of the royal mind was only accidental," but added sarcastically that in the court that accident would soon become a permanent fact (IV, 497). Schlegel also quoted a third source reporting that the king didn't understand *Glauben und Liebe* and asked a member of the court to read it; but he, equally unable to make head or tail of it, had to ask help from someone else. Everybody was curious to know who "Novalis" was, and many suspected one of the Schlegels, for, as Friedrich maliciously remarked, they assumed that everything incomprehensible to them had to be the work of a Schlegel (IV, 497).

Whichever version we accept, Novalis' espousal of monarchy evidently found little sympathy in circles where it should have counted most. But the heated reactions, whether due to incomprehension or genuine disagreement, were to be expected, and *Glauben und Liebe* was destined to become Novalis' most widely discussed work during his life.

As Novalis indicated in the Preface, he was in search of a language of tropes and enigmas comprehensible only to the initiates. He wanted to experiment "whether one could speak one's own language in such a way that only those for whom it was intended would understand it. Every true secret must automatically exclude the profane ones. Whoever understands this secret is, by his own effort, and rightly so, an initiate" (II, 485). But deliberate obscurity was only one of the obstacles to the understanding of *Glauben und Liebe*. A more common source of confusion was that Novalis talked about the real king and existing political institutions to sketch the picture of an ideal court and state, so that it was difficult to say when he referred to the real and when to the ideal. The "facts" of the real court were ultimately unimportant, and Novalis could have used, as Just remarked, the king of Siam as his model (IV, 506). In a sense, the king rightly complained, Novalis projected unto him the image of the ideal ruler, asking him to govern not by power but by virtue of his exemplary character and his capacity to love.

Only he who is already more than a king can regally rule.
Let him then be king who loves the most charming woman. (II, 483)

If the royal couple meets these demands, their marriage and family becomes the microcosm of the ideal state: "Selfless love in the heart and its maxim in the head—that is the only, eternal basis of all true, undissolvable unions. And what is the union of state if not a marriage?" (II, 495)

The conception of the royalty as an exemplary figural head with representative rather than executive functions underlies Novalis' view of the duties of princes and the nature of their court. As already stated in *Blütenstaub*, "most princes were in varying degrees geniuses of their age and appropriately left ruling to subordinates" (II, 445). The king is no "first servant of the state" in the manner of Frederick II (II, 489), but a ceremonial figure who displays value, he is an "artist of artists"—that is a stage director (II, 497).

In emphasizing display and representation, Novalis seems to revert to that concept of "representative publicity" which characterized traditional power: the ruler displays himself and his court through ceremony, festival, and ritual, in order to endow his power with an "aura" and to indicate that his authority is sanctioned from above.[3] But the fundamental difference between medieval and absolutist "representative publicity" on the one hand and Novalis' conception on the other is that Novalis nowhere refers to the divine right of rulers or the relation between human and superhuman power: his discussion is restricted to the sphere of the social and the interpersonal. The moral and religious authority of his ruler is legitimated by his ability to display the potential of his countrymen and exercised through example instead of power. People have "faith" in him not as God's deputy on earth but because, through his exemplary conduct, they can gain faith in the existence of their own, purer self: faith in the divinity is indirect, based on the faith in man's divinity.

Monarchy is the best constitution because it is based "on the belief in a higher born man, on the voluntary adoption of the notion of an ideal man" (II, 489). The king's privileged birth is symbolic of the birth of higher men in future history: "All men should become eligible for the throne. A king is a means of education toward this distant goal" (II, 489). As stated later, we could all be kings if we were not forced to economize (III, 474). Monarchy is therefore a self-destructive institution: through the king's exemplary educational role, ultimately a republic of kings should emerge: "the true king will become a republic, the true republic a king" (III, 490).

That future state is characterized elsewhere as pantheistic (III, 314), because each of its citizens would radiate the genius of the totality.

The king should be an educator and artist. He should attract to his court young military and civil apprentices by founding academies which they will remember with life-long enthusiasm and love: "The noble simplicity of the royal private life, the picture of this happy, intimately united couple would have the most beneficial effect upon the moral education of this 'core of Prussian youth," and thus the king would become the reformer and restorer of his nation and his age (II, 496). The king should become "as many-sided, instructed, well-informed, and free of prejudice, in short, as perfect a man as possible." He should keep abreast of the latest developments in the sciences and the arts, if only by digests and reports, to enable him to give support and encouragement where needed (II, 497).

The primary function of the queen is to embody and to engender love, beauty, and grace, not unlike the medieval mistress, whose educational role was to foster chivalrous *Minne*, a courtly Platonic love. Love for the queen is to counteract the impersonality of modern bureaucracy. Unfortunately, some of the educational functions assigned to the queen foster middle class domesticity: she should set example in the education of her sex, in raising children, in organizing the household, in caring for the sick and the poor, in arranging festivities, but above all in fighting the degradation of her sex in prostitution. Appropriately, the portrait of this paragon of chastity, benevolence, and order is to hang in every young girl's room (II, 493), and her adolescent "apprenticeship" should urgently be recounted in a book (II, 498).

The virtues of the king and the queen should permeate "the great model household," the "enlarged image of classic private life," the court (II, 492). Traditionally eschewed by the virtuous and serious, the court should be purified by the taste of the queen and by her distaste for frivolity, so that young men may once more receive their brides there from her (II, 494).

There is a touch of rococo pastoral and a somewhat tarnished piety in all this, which irritated even some of Novalis' contemporaries, including Friedrich Schlegel. But the sketch offered a point of reference outside history, in terms of which Novalis could articulate a critique of the existing conditions without becoming a defender of the *ancien régime*. Though he preferred monarchy, he did not defend concrete historical manifestations of it, and thus his

critique of republicanism and revolution is unlike Burke's defense
of tradition. As Just remarked, Novalis could fear for his head under
French occupation, but monarchs thinking he was their orthodox
defender would be badly deceived (IV, 505). According to Novalis,
the French king and most princes of Europe had abdicated psy-
chologically and intellectually, if not physically, long before the
French Revolution, for failing as intellectual leaders and molders
of public opinion: "Monarchy ceases to exist where the king is no
longer identical with the intelligence of the state" (II, 492). Similarly, the existing courts fall short of the mark: "With the exception
of theaters and concerts, and occasionally the decoration of rooms,
one finds hardly a trace of taste in the usual European court life"
(II, 493).

If court and royalty fall short of their ideal, mercantilism, democracy, and republicanism are in themselves deficient ideas. Mercantilism may be beneficial for the physical well-being of the state,
but the state is not a factory, and mercantilism therefore endangers
its essence. True patriotism cannot be based on the principle of
self-interest alone (II, 495). Henry IV of France wanted to provide
every citizen with a chicken on Sunday, but Novalis thought that
people would gratefully prefer moldy bread under good government
to roast elsewhere (II, 486). The insatiable pursuit of material wealth
and sensuous pleasure leads to revolution; "only constitutional states
can create enduring happiness. What do all riches help me if they
only stop with me to change horses and complete their trip faster
around the world?" (II, 495).

The weakness of democracy is that it levels everything: "A col-
lapsing throne is like an eroding mountain [. . .] level the mountains, the sea will be grateful to you. The sea is the element of
freedom and equality" (II, 487). "Where the majority decides, power rules over form; the other way round where the minority has the
upper hand," Novalis had noted already in "Vermischte Bemerkungen" (II, 466). Yet he was not principally against democracy,
only against those who "apodictically state that republics exist only—
when there are—assemblies (*Primair-versammlungen*) and elec-
tions, directoriums, councils, municipalities, and freedom trees"
(II, 490). Periodic revolutions may be as necessary for the rejuvenation of the spiritual cosmos as natural upheavals and castastrophes
which bring about new climates, new chemical compounds, and
crystalizations. But the crisis ought to be softened and shortened,

and a core of tradition ought to survive; "permanent revolutions" are undesirable (II, 489f.). Ultimately, age, stability, and security should be fused with youth and the search for the new.

The relative merits of democracy and monarchy are weighed with insight in a chain of dialectically argued "Politische Aphorismen" (II, 501f.), which start from the premise that individuals are buffeted by chance and arbitrary power: "In a full-fledged democracy, I am dependent on a great many arbitrary powers, in a representative democracy on fewer, in a monarchy on a single one." This would give monarchy the edge, except that, according to Kantian principles, men ought to be subject to their reason only. The conflict of both democracy and monarchy is resolvable only if, in Kant's sense, lawgivers as well as citizens overcome their private desires and assert the universal principles of reason, so that positive law and private intention coincide: "Each true law is my law—no matter who states and establishes it" (II, 501). As Novalis remarked later, once the universal laws are internalized, positive laws become superfluous (III, 284f.). The proper state depends on the individuals' ability to overcome their limitations and develop their "universal self."

But wouldn't representative democracy be the best form of government if the ideal ruler was, as Novalis recognized, as yet a "poet's dream?" The next aphorism, attributed to a fictional interlocutor, suggests that the place of the inexistent ideal ruler be taken by a community of less than ideal men, whose talent may constitute a collective artificial intelligence and satisfy the need for ideal representation (II, 502). But ideal rulers and ideal collective leadership are equally illusory. Our states, Novalis had remarked already in the Fichte studies, "are mere agglomerations," while true states are infused with a unifying ideal imagination (II, 290f.). Out of "unjust, selfish, and one-sided men, no just, selfless, and liberal man can be constructed. A majority of as yet morally deficient men will not elect the best but, as a rule, those "for whom mediocrity has become perfectly natural" and those "who know how to court the great crowd." "No spirit will kindle here—least of all a pure one—a great mechanism will form, a bureaucracy (*Schlendrian*), which only intrigue will penetrate occasionally. The reigns of government are going to shift back and forth between [those who insist on] the letter of the law and the multitude of partisans." (II, 502).

Novalis' perceptive criticism of representative democracy, written without any firsthand experience, must be read in light of his less clear-sighted and prophetic diagnosis of dictatorships. He knew that "the ideal of morality has no more dangerous a rival than the ideal of greatest strength" (II, 576); and he recognized, of course, that kings can become "sultans" (II, 499f.). But he considered the despotism of a single person to be preferable to the short-lived petty despotism of bureaucrats in a democracy, because in dealing with the despotism of monarchy, one can "at least save time and shoes"; tyranny "plays with open cards," while in the despotism of democracy one has a hard time finding out "who steers the government at any given day and what ways are most advantageous to reach him" (II, 502f.). The comment on democratic bureaucracy may be valid, but Novalis' patriarchal conception of single man rule prevented him from envisioning a rapid sequence of coup d'etats and dictators and that recent form of impersonal dictatorship where the individual no longer has access to the seat of power, only to frightened subordinates who are unable and unwilling to make decisions. The world of Kafka's *Trial* and *Castle* could be a monarchy as well as a republic.

Novalis must have been aware that these remarks compare the worst of democracy with ideal monarchy. But ultimately, the constitution mattered less to him than the transformation of the individual: "If people were already what they should be and could become—all forms of government would be equal—mankind would be ruled everywhere the same way, everywhere according to the fundamental laws of humanity" (II, 503). Appropriately, the concluding *summa* of *Glauben und Liebe* outlines a mentality indifferent to constitutions:

At least one should be politically as well as religiously tolerant—one should allow for the possibility that even reasonable beings could have dispositions different from ours. It seems to me that this tolerance gradually leads to the sublime conviction that all positive forms are relative—and to the true independence of a mature mind from all individual forms, which to him are but unavoidable means. The time must come when political entheism [monarchy] and pantheism [democracy] will be intimately linked as necessary complementaries. (II, 503).

This offers a critique of historical reality in light of a vision of tolerance—a vision Novalis treasured too much to subject it to compromise and political manipulation. He did not see that democracy is preferable not as the best government among already "transformed" individuals, but as a governance that can grant relative, restricted freedom and independence to people as they exist here and now. Novalis' personal decision was to accept and work for the world given to him, even though it offered less freedom than democracy, because he came to recognize that the freedom he wanted was limited to art, where he was free to create free beings. The decision was not unreasonable and not taken by Novalis alone; but it contributed to one of modern Germany's most serious and chronic problems—namely, that too many of its best minds had only contempt for the partial solutions of the political arena, leaving it thereby prey for the demagogues and the power hungry. When Friedrich Schlegel asked his friend not to squander his faith and love in the political world, but to sacrifice his innermost to "the divine world of science and art, in the sacred firestream of eternal education," Novalis replied on the margin of the manuscript: "I follow these words, dear friend" (III, 492).

III *Thoughts on Religion*

That Hardenberg Senior should have imposed a strict religiosity upon his household with all the fanaticism of a convert did surely more harm than good to his son's religious disposition. While Novalis formally accepted pietism, his personal belief developed only once Sophie's death forced him to reflect seriously about the ultimate questions of life. But the faith that emerged during 1797 and 1798 became highly unorthodox and eclectic because it fed on such diverse sources as the classicism of Hemsterhuis, the pantheism of Spinoza, the pietism of Zinzendorf, and the idealism of Kant and Fichte. The liberality of that faith is perhaps most evident in the lengthy seventy-fourth fragment of *Blütenstaub* (II, 441–45), a key document of Novalis' religious development.

The fragment asserts that finite and fallible man needs to be linked to the infinite Godhead by a mediator. Novalis thought that all men ought to choose freely their mediator, though he recognized that in most cases, ancestry determined the choice. Fetishes, stars, and animals are the least satisfactory mediators, a divine-human monotheistic mediator is the best; the quality of a religion is ultimately determined not by the choice of the mediator, but by the human attitude toward him. Idolatry is to regard the godhead itself as mediator; irreligion is to have no mediator at all; true religion is to regard the mediator as a representative, a concrete appearance of the godhead. According to Novalis, there are only two forms of genuine religion: in pantheism, anything may be chosen as mediator; in monotheism, God reveals himself only through his chosen mediator, whom we are therefore obliged to accept. (The use of the term "pantheism" is somewhat misleading here, for Novalis obviously does not mean an identity between nature and God, for then no mediator would be needed. He must regard the world divine and yet God transcendent.) According to the final postulate, a synthesis between pantheistic free choice and monotheistic necessity should be achieved by placing the monotheistic mediator into the center of all the possible pantheistic choices.

For Novalis, pantheism represents, then, an alternative to monotheism as well as to Fichte's philosophy. But as an alternative to Fichte's self-assertion Spinozism was a submission to the inevitable, while as an alternative to monotheism pantheism offered a freedom of choice. The two apparently incompatible notions of pantheism are both based on the conviction that everything is divine, nothing is fallen from grace; this sacredness of everything justifies, in the first case, the submission to nature's determinism, in the second, the freedom to choose anything as mediator. The reconciliation of pantheism and monotheism presumably means that while all things are divine, one should elect as mediator that which the monotheistic religion designates—that is, one should freely choose what is required. Spinoza's free acceptance of the inevitable was indeed the subject of admiration in Schelling's letters on *Dogmatismus und Kriticismus* (*Dogmatism and Criticism*, 1795), a work that Novalis read after Sophie's death. That sympathy for pantheism was shared by many others, including Goethe, Hölderlin, Friedrich Schlegel, Schleiermacher, as well as Wordsworth, Coleridge, Shelley, and Keats.[4] For Novalis, as we shall see, pantheism served as a theoretical underpinning for the eroticism of his poetry: surrender to the desires of the flesh was not a debasement of human dignity, as the dominant Christian tradition had asserted, but a surrender to an omnipresent divinity.

Novalis formulated these abstract ideas in no small part to answer concrete problems in his life. Choosing Sophie as a bride was already in service of self-development. Her ineluctable death gave Novalis the opportunity to choose her once more, this time as his mediator.

As her image gradually detached itself from her flesh and blood, it gained a new life as redeemer, guardian, intermediary, and inspiration, a role similar to Beatrice's in Dante's life. (The comparison with Dante, first made by Tieck, became popular with later critics such as Carlyle and Maeterlinck.) This freely chosen mediator was then symbolically merged with the mediator of Christianity in the *Hymnen an die Nacht*, where the beloved, Christ, and the Mother blend into each other as complementary mediators of the night, the grave, and the unseen world. Finally, in *Die Christenheit oder Europa*, Christianity oddly assumes as a main feature the "pantheistic" belief in the "total capability *(Allfähigkeit)* of all earthly things to be wine and bread of eternal life" (III, 523).

Could this faith still be called Christian? Having read *Blütenstaub* and *Glauben und Liebe*, Just concluded that Novalis talked about religion in the manner of Kant: "both of you retain the vocabulary of the Christian system of religion and attribute to it a different meaning" (IV, 506). Novalis replied by distinguishing Just's faith from his own. Just's faith was based on his "sympathetic intellect," which accepted the Bible as a pledge of God and immortality and constructed a theology on the basis of a historic-critical understanding of it. But such evidence could not match the religious assurance of Novalis' "sympathetic imagination." He was more inclined to trace the "higher influences" in himself than in historical events and documents. In the history and teaching of the Christian religion, he saw merely the symbolic model of a world religion to come (IV, 272).

The passage is significant for two major reasons. First, by designating the imagination as the faculty and source of religion, Novalis interlinks poetry and religion. Since he had earlier trained his imagination to produce both poetic and religious visions, now it became natural for him to formulate his religious credo in poetic form and, vice versa, to make poetry serve his religious disposition. Second, the passage reveals that, for Novalis, religion was not primarily a product of tradition or a social fact but an imaginative power shaping the future. His correspondence with Friedrich Schlegel shows that in the latter half of 1798, he came to appreciate Christianity precisely because he thought it demanded a revolutionary reorientation in preparing the millennial future. On May 28, Schlegel wrote that he accepted Novalis' notion of mediation, especially for what it implied about the freedom of choice (IV, 494).[5] On

December 2, he remarked that the mediator was for him "pure history" but for Novalis "praxis"—evidently meaning that for Novalis the designation of Sophie as mediator was a practical as well as a theoretical problem. This, Schlegel thought, was a positive view of Christianity, and the question now was whether Novalis could posit it "absolutely negatively, at least in a certain sense" (IV, 508). Novalis responded with an entry in the "Brouillon" (III, 469) which he subsequently included in his reply to Friedrich: "Your idea about the negativity of the Christian religion is excellent. Christianity will thereby become [. . .] the projecting force of a new world-structure and mankind. [. . .] absolute abstraction—annihilation of the present—apotheosis of the future—of this actual, better world, that is the essence of Christianity's message" (IV, 273f.).

"Annihilation of the present" has evidently a double meaning here: first, it refers to the termination of earthly life and the onset of afterlife; second, it designates that revolutionary reorganization of society which will eventually lead to the millennial termination of history. The first of these meanings is essentially the subject of the *Hymnen an die Nacht;* the second is incorporated in *Die Christenheit oder Europa*, where religion, the "new founder of the world," is seen to raise its head from "the destruction of everything positive" (III, 517). Indeed, Schlegel answered by urging Novalis to elaborate on the ideas discussed:

I agree with you that Christianity is a religion of the future, whereas Greek religion was, already in antiquity, one of the past. But is it not even more a religion of death, as classical religion was one of life? [. . .] This must approximately be your opinion as well. If only you could gather once your opinion of Christianity into a single focus! Perhaps you are the first man of our age to have an artistic sense for death. (IV, 525)

Schlegel's urging that Novalis make use of his "artistic sense for death" was probably prompted by his conversations with the theologian Friedrich Schleiermacher, who was at the time finishing his speeches *Über die Religion (On Religion)*. As the subtitle states, Schleiermacher addressed himself to the "Educated Disdainers" of religion, foremost among them the artists, whom he wanted to regain for the cause of religion. He tried to free religion from dogma, tradition, or institutions on the one hand and from philosophy and morality (thought and action) on the other and to define it as a "sense and taste for the infinite," whose "most general and highest formula" was the "contemplation of the universe."[6]

Thus, Schleiermacher stripped religion of its trappings and brought it into the vicinity of Novalis' notion of a poetic sense. He believed that a religious mind can only be formed by a free contemplation of some aspect of the universe which could then be taken as the point of reference and the source of religious inspiration[7]— a striking parallel to Novalis' intention to relate everything to Sophie (IV, 37). Schleiermacher counted poets, seers, speakers, and artists among the "true priests of the highest", because "after each excursion of their spirit into infinity," they could communicate their experiences "in words or images."[8] Thus, to Schleiermacher, as to Novalis, the poet was a mystic, a priest, and a prophet, and Schleiermacher could celebrate the artists as inadvertent saviors and cultivators of religion because he thought that great art more than anything else fostered the sense for the universe.[9]

Schleiermacher's call for a return to a more essential faith, and his espousal of an "art-religion" (III, 562) were so congenial to Novalis that he was "completely taken, penetrated, enthused, and enflamed" when he read *Über die Religion* in September 1799. He claimed to be in complete agreement with it and promised Schlegel to write a kindred essay on Catholicism (IV, 641), by which he probably meant his *Christenheit*. Schleiermacher's *Über die Religion* was to be celebrated there as a "solemn call to a new primordial assembly, as a powerful wing-stroke of a passing angelic herald" (III, 521). *Christenheit* did not quite satisfy Schleiermacher because he thought that the papacy was the ruin of Catholicism,[10] but he retained a deep respect for Novalis and added to the 1815 edition of his work a passage in which he lamented the early death of the "divine young man" and concluded: "When all philosophers shall be religious and seek for God, like Spinoza, and all artists shall be pious and love Christ, like Novalis, then will the mighty resurrection of both worlds be initiated."

IV   Die Christenheit oder Europa

Novalis' renewed interest in Christianity was kindled by his admiration for Raphael's Sistine Madonna in the Dresden Art Gallery, his correspondence with Schlegel about the "absolute negativity of Christianity," and Schleiermacher's *Über die Religion. Christenheit*

oder Europa was also a response to important historical events.
After the second sacking of Rome, the Vatican was turned into a
republic; when Pope Pius VI died in exile on August 29, 1799, no
successor could be elected, and as Novalis remarks, the papacy lay
in its grave (III, 524). On October 9, Napoleon returned from his
Egyptian campaign to save France from its crisis, quickly overthrew
the Directorate, and seized sole power on November 9, the day
Novalis completed his speech. It was meant to persuade, in the face
of the unmistakable contrast between declining sacred and rising
secular powers, that only the supranational spiritual power of a new
"Christendom" could resolve the power struggle of "Europe."[12]

The structure of the essay is determined by Novalis' triadic conception of history: a state of harmony is followed by disunity, which
must, however, lead back to a higher peace. We shall recognize
this scheme in the *Hymnen an die Nacht* and the inserted tales of
Heinrich von Ofterdingen as well. In *Christenheit*, the "beautiful,
resplendent days" of the early Middle Ages form the first stage, the
evolution of the modern world the second, and the vision of a
millennial age the final one. The speech is given at a moment of
transition from the second to the third period, when the formative
forces of the future are just emerging from the depth of crisis: "true
anarchy is the breeding ground of religion" (III, 517). Its largest
part is taken up by the decline in the middle period, which led to
the problems of the speaker's age. Accordingly, the paragraphs of
the essay describe the unified Europe under the church (1–2), the
decline of the medieval culture and the destructive effects of reformation (3–8), the counterreformation of the Jesuits (9), the enlightenment (10–11), the age of revolutionary events (12–20), and
finally, the dawn of the new age (21–30).

The picture of medieval unity is deliberately kept vague by the
absence of dates and names: language and style evoke a mythical
childhood. The church, the priests, and the pope were "experienced
navigators," whom men trusted with a childlike faith. Protected
men led a peaceful life and possessed a serenity gained in "the
beautiful assemblies in the mysterious churches, which were
adorned with uplifting pictures, filled with sweet fragrances, and
animated by sacred and exalting music" (III, 508). The church rightly preferred infinite faith to a limited scientific knowledge that en-
dangered religious harmony.

The speaker locates three major causes for the decline of this golden age: first, man was not yet "mature and educated" enough for it (but immaturity was, of course, necessary in order to have a childlike faith!); second, introspective spirituality was perhaps smothered by the communal spirit ("a certain solitude seems to be necessary for the prosperity of the higher senses"); third, since history is change, growth and flowering had to be followed by decline ("faith and love," the "beautiful flowers of its youth," are replaced by "the coarser fruits of knowing and possessing") (III, 510).

The church weakened first because of internal secularization and the decline of the priesthood: "the actual rule of Rome had silently ceased to exist long before the violent insurrection" (III, 510f.) The insurgent "protestants" introduced many healthy and beneficial changes. Adopting an Erasmian position, the speaker asserts, however, that "they separated the inseparable, divided the indivisible church and sacrilegiously tore themselves loose from the universal Christian community through which, and in which alone, true and enduring rebirth was possible" (III, 511). Reformation's unfortunate consequence was to apportion religion among the secular powers; its fatal mistake was to base faith on "the sacred universality of the Bible" and thus to inject into it an alien, earthly discipline, namely, philology (III, 512). We have to remember Novalis' insistence on the distinction between the spirit and letter in order to understand this startling assertion. Textual exegesis can satisfy only those for whom the Bible is "a pledge of God and immortality." For Novalis, textual studies emphasized literality at the cost of the spirit, and "this choice was highly injurious to the religious sense, for nothing destroys its sensibility more than the letter" (III, 512). As a consequence of this scholarly and sober approach to religion, the protestant burst of holy fire soon led to a "dessication of the sacred sense," and only the flashes of a Zinzendorf or a Jakob Boehme followed. The Reformation led to the period of "practical disbelief": "Christendom was over [. . .] Catholics, Lutherans, and Calvinists stood further apart in sectarian isolation than Mohamedans and heathens" (III, 513).

The most controversial part of the speech was its praise for the founding of the Jesuit order as a valiant effort to overcome the protestant schism, since the order was at the time suspended and universally disliked. "Never before had a greater intelligence applied itself to a greater idea" (III, 513) the speaker asserts; science,

worldwide missionary activity, powerful rhetoric, and care for education were hallmarks of an order of "poets and philosophers,
ministers and martyrs." Since the Jesuits maintained a consistency
of action and doctrine during their tremendous expansion (III, 514),
they serve as an eternal model for all societies "that feel an organic
yearning after endless expansion and infinite duration" (III, 513).
This admiration is tempered, however, by the speaker's awareness
that no such "duration" is possible in history, that no human intervention can alter its organic and inevitable changes. The story
of the Jesuits proves "that unguarded time alone undoes the cleverest enterprises and that the natural growth of the entire species
incessantly suppresses the artificial growth of any part" (III, 513f.).
Perhaps the time of the Jesuits has not yet come: "Now the fearful
order sleeps in destitute form on the outskirts of Europe [Prussia
and Russia]; perhaps from there [. . .] it will some day spread with
new force over its old homeland" (III, 514).

The praise of the learned Jesuits is followed by a scathing con-
demnation of modern secular learning. "If scholars and priests are
separated, they must wage a deadly war because they vie for one
and the same position" (III, 515); thus scholars gained ground as
mankind embraced triumphant science, and knowledge became an
opponent of faith. The hate for Catholicism extended first to Christianity, then to religion in general, and finally to all objects of
enthusiasm. The resultant Deism and Mechanism are portrayed by
the speaker with a magnificent image: secular knowledge "turned
the infinite creative music of the cosmos into the monotonous clatter
of a monstrous mill, which, driven by the stream of chance and
floating on it, was supposed to be a mill-in-itself without builder or
miller, actually a true perpetuum mobile, a self-milling mill" (III,
515). The enthusiasm for rationality, enlightenment's only permis-
sible enthusiasm, led to an all-out effort to cleanse the world of
poetry, "to obliterate every trace of the sacred, to discredit sarcastically the memory of all uplifting events and persons." In Germany especially an effort was made to replace religious awe and
wonder, marvel and mystery, by a modern, rational, and trivial
concept of the divinity: "God was turned into an idle spectator of
the great sentimental show staged by the scholars" (III, 516).

According to the speaker, this "history of modern disbelief"
inevitably led to a "second, more comprehensive and characteristic
Reformation," the French Revolution. As a crowning achievement

of the Enlightenment which whipped up the emotions and thereby made a renewal of religious enthusiasm possible, the revolution was the point of dialectical inversion: "the time of [revolutionary] resurrection has come [. . .] just those events which [. . .] threatened to complete [religion's] complete destruction, have become the most favorable signs of its regeneration" (III, 517). The "state topplers" are like Sisyphus: their mighty burden will not stay in equipoise unless "an attraction to heaven keeps it hovering in the altitude"—that is, unless the earth-bound, secular state is infused with a religious spirit reaching out for the universe in Schleiermacher's sense. But this transformation of the political revolution into a great spiritual renewal must come by itself, for history is "independent" and "self-willed" (III, 518). Sure signs of a new world, especially in Germany, indicate to the speaker that this "second reformation" is not going to get stuck with the letter like the first one. While the other European countries "are occupied with war, speculation, and partisan spirit," the Germans industriously work toward a "higher epoch of culture." Scientists reexamine the objects, writers become more individualistic and powerful; "a tremendous intimation of inner humanity's creative freedom, boundlessness, infinite multiplicity, sacred individuality, and omnipotence seems to be astir everywhere" (III, 519). Accordingly, the speaker assumes a biblical and visionary tone to portray a universal reconciliation, a victory of poetry over learning, and the birth of a "new golden age."

The first stage of reconciliation is to recognize the historical role and significance of the immediate past: "We now stand high enough to offer a friendly smile to the above-mentioned preceding times [. . .] for this obsession had to exhaust itself for the sake of the descendants, and the scientific view of the objects had to establish itself" (III, 520). The future poetic world is now portrayed in a new poetic language of metaphors: a life in warm and "adorned India" will be possible due to the cold, frigid sea, the dead cliffs, and the fog at the other ends of the pole—the mistakes of the past. The scientists, men of letters, philosophers, and encyclopedists, possess "cold, lifeless, icy peaks of bookish intellect," they are the "anchorites" in the "deserts of intellect" who led a life of self-denial, misguidedly pursued secular knowledge; they must now be greeted to a friendlier climate. Since this invitation to the intellectuals echoes Schleiermacher's appeal to them, it is appropriate that the speaker should lead his audience to a "brother," a "heartbeat of the new age," whose words will make their heart leap. The new veil of this "veil-maker" (Schleier-macher)—namely, his *Über die Religion,*—drapes and yet chastely reveals the contours of the coming sacred age.

The "highest in natural philosophy" functions as another sign of the approaching future. The unity of the sciences inspired attempts to mystify them; philosophy, that pure representation of the scientific method, became "the symmetric foundation of the sciences" (through Kant, Fichte, and Schelling) (III, 521); while scientists like Werner "established new relations between the concrete sciences, promoted a lively interchange among them, and attempted to clarify their classification in natural history" (III, 52f.).

The speaker sees the political situation in analogy to that of science: the upheaval may establish multiple relations between the European states and, from these, a "state of states," a political equivalent to Fichte's "science of science" *(Wissenschaftslehre).* If the "symmetric foundation" of science is a Fichtean theory of knowledge, "the principle of federation among states" may be hierarchy, that "intellectual intuition of the political self" (III, 522). Although the speaker seems to accept a hierarchy of political power comparable to the structure of the Catholic church, he believes that "secular forces cannot be in equilibrium, only a third element, which is at once secular and otherworldly, can solve this task [. . .] from the perspective of cabinets and the common mind no agreement is conceivable" (III, 522). In yearning for a spiritual power capable of offering the palm branch of peace, the speaker evokes the pious religion of medieval Catholicism portrayed at the outset, admitting however that the "accidental"—that is, historical—form of Catholicism is "as good as annihilated" (III, 524). True Christianity will reappear in a triple form, as the creative power and joy of all religions, as the religion of mediation (all earthly things are capable of becoming the "wine and bread of eternal life!"), and as the specifically Catholic belief in Christ, the Madonna, and the saints. The new spiritual power will therefore be ecumenical: "Choose whichever you wish, choose all three, it makes no difference; you will thereby become Christians and members of a single, eternal, unspeakably happy community" (III, 523). The final millennial vision is based on the Book of Revelations (20–21): during the "sacred age of eternal peace, New Jerusalem will be the capital of the world," a visible church of supranational Christendom will embrace "all souls thirsting for the supernatural, and gladly become the mediator between the old and the new world" (III, 524).

When Novalis read the speech to his friends in August Wilhelm Schlegel's house in November 1799, the reactions were negative. Dorothea Schlegel reported to Schleiermacher that Christianity was the order of the day and the gentlemen were somewhat crazy (IV, 647), and even her husband, Friedrich, shared Schelling's "new fit of old enthusiasm for irreligion," expressed in Schelling's witty parody of *Christenheit*, entitled *Epikurisch Glaubensbekenntnis Heinz Widerporstens (Heinz Widerporsten's Epicurean Confession of Faith)* (IV, 646). Novalis took Schelling's repartee in good spirit and consented to the plan to print *Christenheit* and its parody side by side in the *Athenäum*, but the editors had second thoughts and finally decided against publication, at Goethe's advice. Tieck, who found the "historical perspective too weak and insufficient, the deductions too arbitrary, and the whole essay too feeble" (III, 500), included only eight passages from the work in his first three Novalis editions, so that the full text appeared only in the 1826 edition.

Together with Wackenroder's writings, with Tieck's *Franz Sternbalds Wanderungen (Franz Sternbald's Wanderings)* and Novalis' own Madonna poems, *Christenheit* was among the first sympathetic reappraisals of Catholicism at the end of the eighteenth century, and it is understandable therefore that even Just considered Novalis a "panegyrist of papal autocracy" (IV, 541). But due to the late publication of the full text, the essay couldn't have played a significant role in the Catholic tendencies of later German Romanticism. Neither can the charge of Wilhelm Dilthey and others be substantiated that Novalis anticipated the Holy Alliance and clothed it in a Christian garb,[13] for neither the speaker's portrayal of the past nor his vision of the future fit the Holy Alliance. He expressly says that policies formulated by cabinets and based on notions of power—the kind of diplomacy practiced by Metternich—could never lead to the imaginary "state of state." While the speaker envisions a "venerable European council" from whose "holy womb" Christendom shall emerge (III, 524), he does not conceive of it as a defender of the status quo or as a means of restoration, but as an arbitrator between "the ineradicable powers of the human heart"—namely, the love of tradition and the spirit of innovation and freedom (III, 522f.). Its "comprehensive divine plan" will eliminate protest "against Christian and secular compulsion, for the essence of the church will be freedom and all necessary reforms will be carried out under its leadership as peaceful and formal affairs of the state" (III, 524).

The visionary future cannot be understood, therefore, as a mere resurrection of any historical past; until the arrival of the millennial period, historical change is irreversible, ceaseless, and inevitable. Medieval culture had to decline because "oscillation, an alternation of contrary movements" is the essence of history; Reformation was a "sign of the time" (III, 515); the Jesuits failed because "the cleverest enterprises" cannot succeed against the "natural growth of the entire species" (III, 513f.); revolution is a "foolish endeavor" to give self-willed history a man-willed direction (III, 518). In a Hegelian sense of history, even "the odd follies" of the enlightenment are necessary and ultimately beneficial, for they reveal "remarkable crystallizations of the historical material" (III, 520).

Thus, utopian, progressive, and conservative elements intermingle in the speaker's conception of history.[14] But in contrast to Novalis' earlier conviction that man molds his fate by a creative use of his faculties, the speech assigns a passive role to man. History is now "a gospel" (III, 565), an unfolding of a divine plan for the healing of man. Since history is preordained and organic, a revolutionary intervention and transformation is impossible. The purpose of studying history is not to change its course but merely to understand it, to search for its "instructive coherence" with the "magic wand of analogy," "to follow its ways, to learn from it, to keep step with it, to follow its promises and hints with faith" (III, 518). The closing vision of a New Jerusalem is conceived, therefore, not as a call for action but as an exhortation to patient and passive preparation: "When and how soon? Do not ask. Have patience, it will, it must come, that sacred time of eternal peace [. . .] until then be serene and courageous amidst the dangers of time. Brothers in faith, proclaim with word and deed the divine gospel and remain loyal to the true eternal faith until your death" (III, 524).[15] This reflects no satisfaction with the present, only a belief in the inevitability of the future. While it is a counsel for political inaction, it does ask for "word and deed" to spread the gospel; and the speech must therefore be understood as an example of such symbolic action. It was not conceived as a mosaic of facts, an objective piece of historiography, but rather as a rhetorical argument to convince the audience that history is pregnant with portents of the millennial future. While the text seems to buttress a vision with historical evidence, logically and rhetorically it projects aspects of that vision upon the historical past: the speaker glorifies Christianity and Catholicism because they come closest to the ecumenical and spiritual power he envisions. Historical inaccuracy will become of secondary importance if we conceive of the speaker as a visionary and rhetorician rather than a historian: "The historian must become a speaker in his presentation. He presents gospels because all history is a gospel" (III, 586).

Indeed, Novalis probably regarded the speech as a rhetorical exercise.[16] At the time, he was interested in the nature and structure of speeches and noted that "in a true speech one must play all roles"; a speech is a "monologue drama" in which the speaker "must be able to assume every tone" (III, 649). When the work was rejected, he planned to include it in a volume of speeches (IV, 317). Indeed, the text modulates between biblical, lyric, ironic, hymnic, and dramatic tones, between short and long sentences, and between a monologue and dialogue form of address. The metaphoric and rhetorical features of the speech should not overshadow its message, but they should remind us that the communicated truth belongs to the imagination rather than to history and politics.

CHAPTER 6

The Lyric Poet

I Hymnen an die Nacht

THE *Hymnen* are Novalis' major completed poetic work, which ranks with the poetry of Blake, Wordsworth, Coleridge, Keats, Goethe, Hölderlin, or Leopardi. In the history of German poetry perhaps only Hölderlin's last hymns and Rilke's *Duineser Elegien (Duino Elegies)* can match their majestic yet personal tone. But they have stimulated more indiscriminate adulation and less intelligent criticism than Wordsworth's *Prelude*, Coleridge's "Kubla Khan," or Keats' odes, and they have not attracted as good poet-translators as did Hölderlin's odes and Rilke's elegies. Carlyle, whose essay on Novalis contains a translation of the third hymn, was puzzled rather than overwhelmed by them; he found there a "vastness, an immensity of idea" and thought that "a still solemnity [. . .] a solitude almost as of extinct worlds" reigned in them— but ultimately they appeared veiled and enigmatic to him.[1] The inadequacy of translations is both a sign of and a reason for the neglect of Novalis' hymns among English-speaking readers.

A major problem seems to be that the last two of the six hymns are quite different from the first four in style and content. The first hymns contain a highly rhythmic prose monologue of a lonely speaker to whom the departed beloved appears under the guise of the night in a vision. Subsequently he must learn to reconcile the continued demands of life with his yearning for a reunification in death. In the last two hymns, written almost completely in verse, that individual experience gains new, Christian meaning: by shifting from the beloved to Christ and the Holy Mother, Christianity becomes the religion of night and death. The theme of death links the first and the second part, and the historical interpretation of Christianity gives a transindividual answer to the individual predicament. The hymnic tone of the opening and the songlike simplicity of the final hymn are admirable, each in their own way, but the intervening stylistic fissure and thematic refocusing disorient the reader's sensibility, especially if he can no longer give intellectual assent to the resolution of the last hymns. For many modern readers, a full response to the cycle will literally demand a "willing suspension of disbelief."

The *Hymnen* were published in the August 1800 issue of the *Athenäum*. The only surviving draft (="h") was probably written a few months before Novalis dispatched the final manuscript in February 1800. Since the first three hymns of "h" contain few corrections and the last ones many, earlier drafts probably existed for the former but not for the latter. The crucial change between "h" and the final version was that, for reasons unknown, Novalis decided to print hymns I–III and large segments of V in a revolutionary prose poem format.

Sophie's death was not the cause of but an opportunity for the release of Novalis' poetic energies. The diary was the first effort to endow death with meaning by reinterpreting the unalterable fact as an ethical as well as an aesthetic calling to reorient his life, mold his character, and exercise his imagination. As the diary recorded Novalis' spiritual turmoil and simultaneously represented a product of it, so the *Hymnen* are a symbolic autobiography which portrays the struggle for a Christian faith and the emergence of the hymn cycle itself. Religious and aesthetic intents are in mutual support, because both of them rest on the working of the imagination and memory, both of them are products of a long, reflective process. If the portrayal of an emerging religious spirituality relies on a long tradition, the idea of writing a poem cycle essentially about its own making is distinctly modern: the *Hymnen* are at the watershed between tradition and modernity, belonging to both of them in a unique way. The cycle opens with a majestic praise of light:

Welcher Lebendige, Sinnbegabte, liebt nicht vor allen Wundererscheinungen des verbreiteten Raums um ihn, das allerfreuliche Licht. (I, 131)

(What living sense-endowed being loves not most among all the wonders in spread out space around him, light that gives joy to all.)

The sight rapidly sweeps over the light-enjoying beings: the cosmic world of restless stars ("der rastlosen Gestirne Riesenwelt"), the sensuous sucking plant ("die sinnige, saugende Pflanze"), the wild, burning, multiformed animal ("das wilde, brennende, vielgestaltete Tier"), and finally man, the magnificent stranger ("der herrliche Fremdling") in the realm of light.

The praise of light proves to be a rhetorical inversion when the speaker turns to "the sacred, ineffable, and mysterious night," associated with inwardness, memory, childhood dreams, and desires, but also with intoxication and sensuous pleasure. This lonely realm first engenders only a desire to regain light, but when night's black cloak reveals opium, darkness is accepted. In the fading starlight, reminder of daylight, the inner eyes perceive a bright, loving face that fills "higher space" and offers unspeakable pleasures. The hymn culminates in a celebration of the night as the queen of the world and guardian of the lovers' union. As night's "lovely sun," the beloved ignites life-consuming and sustaining ecstasy: "zehre mit Geisterglut meinen Leib, daβ ich luftig mit dir inniger mich mische und dann ewig die Brautnacht währt" (I, 133: "consume my body with spectral fire that I may mingle airily and more intimately with you, and the nuptial night may last then forever").

In explicit contrast to the opening praise of light, the second hymn starts with a lament about its inevitable return. Light, the rational, life-affirming power, is now subservient to the eternal and spaceless imperium of the night, of which "the golden flood of grapes" and the "brown juice of poppies" are harbingers. (I, 133).

The third hymn abruptly shifts to the portrayal of a vision at the grave of a departed lover. The thematic contrast between nocturnal intoxication and daylight clarity continues when the "barren mound which sheltered in a narrow dark space the figure of my life" (I, 135) becomes the scene of the central vision recorded in the diary.

But how is life to continue once a momentary ecstasy has revealed a higher mode of existence? The general affirmation of the night must now lead to concrete advice on how to live in the shadow of death. The answer of the fourth hymn is first suggested by an association between the grave of the beloved and the holy grave, which points toward a Christian interpretation of the personal experience, though the new life does not as yet have a specifically Christian character:

Die kristallene Woge, die gemeinen Sinnen unvernehmlich, in des Hügels dunkeln Schoβ quillt, an dessen Fuβ die irdische Flut bricht, wer sie gekostet, wer oben stand auf dem Grenzgebürge der Welt, und hinübersah in das neue Land, in der Nacht Wohnsitz—wahrlich der kehrt nicht in das Treiben der Welt zurück, in das Land, wo das Licht in ewiger Unruh hauset. (I, 137)

(The crystal wave, which, imperceptible to common senses, springs forth in the dark womb of that hill at whose foot the earthly tide breaks—whoever tasted it, stood up there at the mountainous divide of the world and looked into the new country, the seat of the night—truly he will not return to the bustle of the world where light dwells in eternal restlessness.)

A passage of poignant beauty follows: those who had the visionary experience will build their huts of peace on the ridge between life and death and peer from there into the yonder until the desired hour comes. The earthly remains will then be washed back into the realm of the living, while the parts anointed by love will lose their substantiality by flowing into the yonder, dissolving into scent, and finally mingling with the beloved.

This ultimate loyalty to the other world allows the cheerful execution of earthly duties and encourages the self to confront the day with the warning that its power is ephemeral against eternal night, the true abode of the self. The cross emerges as the pledge of the irresistible final victory of the "old magnificent heaven": "Unburnable stands the Cross—a victory standard of our race" (I, 139). The Christian meaning of the night, suggested in the opening of the fourth hymn by the holiness of the grave, is now explicit. The hymn concludes with two stress verses of remarkable rhythmic power and sensuous imagery:

> Hinüber wall ich,
> Und jede Pein
> Wird einst ein Stachel
> der Wollust sein.
> [. . .]
> O! sauge, Geliebter,
> Gewaltig mich an,
> Daβ ich entschlummern
> Und lieben kann. (I, 139)

(I'll wander to the other side, and every pain will some day be a sting of pleasure [. . .] Oh! suck me with force toward you, beloved, that I may fall into slumber, and love.)

The fifth hymn restates the personal themes on a historical-religious plane. Christianity emerges as the religion that gives meaning to death, and Christ as the guarantor of life beyond death. This hymn, by far the longest, represents a reaction to the "aesthetic paganism" of late eighteenth-century classicism which started with the archeological work of Johann Joachim Winckelmann and culminated with Goethe and Schiller. Novalis' interpretation of Greek culture is actually a direct response to Schiller's famous poem "Die Götter Griechenlands" *(The Gods of Greece)* (1788), a poem which, back in 1790, he wanted to defend against charges of atheism. The hymn opens with a joyous festivity amidst Greek gods and men which is interrupted "with fear and pain and tears" (I, 143) by the irrepressible thought of death. For its inability to cope with death, Greek culture had to disappear, nature's gods were replaced by the "barren number and harsh measure," faith and imagination faded. The gods had to withdraw into night's "mighty womb of revelations," (I, 145) waiting for the rejuvenation of the world by the child-savior.

Here Novalis weaves into the hymn the enigmatic legend of a Greek singer who becomes an emissary of the "wondrous child" and moves to Hindostan to spread the joyous message:

> Im Tode war das ewge Leben kund,
> Du bist der Tod und machst uns erst gesund. (I, 147)

(In death eternal life was revealed / Thou art death and only thou canst heal us.)

The poet becomes a missionary whose gospel the hymn itself now announces by giving a symbolic account of Christ's life, death, and resurrection. Following the pattern of the previous hymn, the fifth ends with a verse passage, this time in praise of the Madonna as symbol of the newly won life of love. As a female figure, she links the beloved with Christ and completes the hymns' triumvirate of mediators.

Only the sixth and final hymn is fully in verse and is given a title, "Yearning for Death." The "I" of the first five hymns now changes to "we" to underscore the emergence of a simple, communal, church-song voice.

The stylistic alternations of the cycle roughly correspond to the shifts from prose to verse: hymns I–III, most of IV (except of the

final twenty-eight lines), and parts 1 and 3 of V are in prose; the
major part of V and all of VI in verse. As the cycle progresses, prose
is thus slowly giving way to verse. The highly rhythmic prose contains occasional alliterations and blank verse, but is not reducible
to regular verse. The prose poem form was a new departure in the
history of modern poetry, though it relied on the loosened poetic
form in the odes and hymns of Klopstock and the young Goethe.
Appropriately, the Christian creed is finally reaffirmed in the stricter
form of rhymed verse.

Though the hymnic form asks for a supple flow of language, Novalis does not abandon his preference for short sentences. For instance, the whole middle section of the first hymn consists of short
unconnected pronouncements:

Abwärts wend ich mich zu der heiligen, unaussprechlichen, geheimniß-
vollen Nacht. Fernab liegt die Welt—in eine tiefe Gruft versenkt—wüst
und einsam ist ihre Stelle. In den Saiten der Brust weht tiefe Wehmut.
In Tautropfen will ich hinuntersinken und mit der Asche mich vermischen.
(I, 131)

(Downward I turn to the sacred, ineffable, mysterious night. Far below
lies the world—sunk into a deep tomb—barren and lonely is its place. In
the chords of the heart, profound melancholy wafts. In drops of dew I want
to sink down and mix with the ashes.)

The first and last sections of this hymn contain some longer sentences, but they are generated by enumeration and addition rather
than by complex syntactical organization. Thus, the opening sentence is stretched by the appositive characterization, "light—with
its colors, its beams and waves; its mild omnipresence, as an awakening day" (I, 131); the next sentence is stretched by enumerating
the elements of nature—the stars, the stone, the plant, the animal,
and "the magnificent stranger." The last and longest sentence of
this hymn actually contains several coordinate clauses:

Preis der Weltkönigin, der hohen Verkünderin heiliger Welten, der Pfle-
gerin seliger Liebe—sie sendet mir dich—zarte Geliebte—liebliche Sonne
der Nacht,—nun wach ich—denn ich bin Dein und Mein—du hast die
Nacht mir zum Leben verkündet—mich zum Menschen gemacht [. . .]
(I, 133)

(Praise the world-queen, the high proclaimer of holy worlds, the nurse of
blissful love—she sends you to me—tender beloved—lovely sun of the

night—now I awaken—for I am yours and mine—you have proclaimed that
the night be my life—have made me human [. . .])

Since the hymns contain only few of those complex hypotactical
German sentences which bring despair to translators of Kleist, Schopenhauer, Kafka, or Thomas Mann, they should be relatively easy
to translate—at least as far as syntax is concerned. Causal connec-
tives of subordination, such as "because" *(weil)* or "since" *(da)*, as
well as additive conjunctions of coordination are rare. Novalis' language tends to move by leaps and shifts, so that each statement is
either a new beginning or a variation on the previous one; the
resultant broken discourse harks back to the aphoristic style of the
notes and fragments.

When Novalis occasionally engages in portrayal, the loose, coordinate syntax generates images of quick and slight strokes, but
the lack of visual detail and the quick shifts in perspective do not
allow for clear spatial perception. The medium of the hymns is
remarkably fluid, the contours are vague, and the superposition of
spatially incongruent elements creates a sense of surrealistic semi-
abstraction, of which the pleasures of the night in the first hymn
are representative:

Was quillt auf einmal so ahndungsvoll unterm Herzen, und verschluckt
der Wehmut weiche Luft? Hast auch du ein Gefallen an uns, dunkle Nacht?
Was hältst du unter deinem Mantel, was mir unsichtbar kräftig an die Seele
geht? Köstlicher Balsam träuft aus deiner Hand, aus dem Bündel Mohn.
(I, 131)

(What is welling up suddenly so portentously beneath my heart and swallows up melancholy's soft air? Do you also like us, dark night? What do
you keep under your cloak that invisibly, forcefully encroaches upon my
soul? Precious balsam trickles from your hand, from the sheaf of poppy.)

Three carefully structured questions follow here additively: the
first registers the welling beneath the heart, the second addresses
the night in search of the cause, the third assumes that the night
was responsible for the euphoria but continues the search for the
specific agent. The sequence doesn't proceed by questions and answers but by rhetorical questions which disorient the reader by the
lack of logical development and by the vagueness of the visual
situation, both of which reflect the speaker's drugged mind. This

deliberate disorientation of sense and logic is Novalis' way to force the reader to share the speaker's newly won susceptibility to the night. Stylistically, it is a departure from a Gothean clarity in service of a Rimbaudian "immense and reasoned derangement of all the senses"[2]—except that this derangement fosters sensitivity to Christianity's otherworldly message. The reader's perceptual disorientation is achieved in the quoted passage by the construction of a multidimensional space where objects, perceptions, and metaphors depart from their normal function and transgress into each others' sphere. The phrase "swallows up melancholy's soft air" fuses, for instance, the metaphoric tenor and vehicle in such a way that the two parts become indistinguishable, and this metaphoric construction is linked to *schlucken*, a verb that is normally not applied in German to melancholy or to air. It is impossible and inappropriate to place these words in a coherent spatial order and temporal sequence. Novalis actually remarked that the "negativity of the Christian religion" excellently suited his ideas on space and time because [in Kant's sense] these were human "creative forces" which established the "pivotal points of the world." The creative use of space and time allowed that "absolute abstraction, annihilation of the present, and apotheosis of the future" which he saw as the "essence of Christianity's promise" (IV, 273f.).

The fluid imagery of Novalis' style is reinforced by the remarkable abstraction of his vocabulary. The recurrent motifs and figures of the cycle have hardly any plasticity; the faces of the beloved, Christ, and the Mother may merge because none are portrayed in physical detail. The nouns generally tend to be abstract; many of them are merely adjectival (e.g., *das Irdische* = the terrestrial), and those denoting physical entities are more often than not vague or unassuming, as for instance the following ten nouns that comprise the opening section of the second hymn: morning, the terrestrial, power, bustle, approach, night, love, sacrifice, light, and time.

The higher frequency and intensity of adjectives distinguishes the prose from the verse sections.[3] While twenty-four of the one hundred and seventeen words in the first prose section of Hymn I are adjectives, in the verses of Hymn VI there are only eighteen out of three hundred and fourteen. Furthermore, among the latter, "sweet" occurs three times, "eternally" twice, and the remaining adjectives are mostly such common words as wild, happy, narrow, long, and age-old. These adjectives are joined to equally pale nouns to form a style of modest vocabulary which fades against the sonorous power of the even-measured and rhymed tetrameters: in Hymn VI and the verses of Hymn V, rhythm, rhyme, and lyrical mood dominate over meaning and verbal intensity. The startling and dramatic adjectives of the first hymn yield, on the other hand, a colorful picture full of such bold and idiosyncratic compounds as *allerfreulich* ("giving joy to all"), *ewigruhend* ("eternally resting"), *zartgeschlossen* ("delicately closed"), *vielgestaltet* ("multiform") or *tonreich* ("rich in sounds"). Occasionally, these combinations are further compounded to produce astonishing images: the stone is *funkelnd ewigruhend* ("glittering and eternally at rest"), the plant is *sinnig saugend* ("pensive, sucking"), the animal is *wild, brennend, vielgestaltet* ("wild, burning, multiform"), and finally man has *zartgeschlossene, tonreiche Lippen* ("delicately closed, sound-rich lips"). The effect of these compounds is enhanced by the absence of conjunctions in the adjectival and participial strings.

The opening hymns are characterized, then, by idiosyncratic verbal brilliance, while the final hymn uses a pietist language to express a communal faith. If the powerful language of the first hymn is appropriate to the uneven pulsation of hymnic prose, the simple vocabulary of the sixth hymn accords with the strict meter: the contrasting styles mark the emotional and intellectual terminals of a cycle that moves from a radically individualistic position to the final affirmation of the communal. The merely personal experience broadens into a universal issue through an inversion of Christian mystic eroticism. While mystics see Christ or the Madonna as a lover or bridegroom, Novalis reverses the relationship and projects the beloved upon Christ and the Mother. The metaphoric and implicit eroticism of mystic literature becomes here explicit and literal, as the real lover is the erotic object: Mystic sensuality issues from an intense veneration of the divinity, while Novalis' erotic yearning for the beloved is an occasion for religious experience. The metamorphosis of the personal grave into the holy grave merged the personal into the universal mediator, accommodated Novalis' erotic pantheism within Christianity, and established Christianity as the religion of the future because it held out the hope both for a reunification with the beloved and for a millennial reunion at the terminal point of history. The struggle to understand the lover's death and the search for a faith were therefore interrelated: the loss of the lover was that emotional experience which, for all his pietistic upbringing, Novalis needed to find his faith.

The *Hymnen* can thus be seen as a symbolic spiritual exploration of death in search of a new life. Death was no mere negation of life, but another life beyond those "frontier mountains" that wise men populate according to the fourth hymn. Interlinking life and death in an interior space, Novalis' *Hymnen* bear an affinity with Rilke's *Duineser Elegien* which extends over a whole network of themes and images. If the *Elegien* do not end with an affirmation of Christianity, the credo emerging from the *Hymnen* is highly unorthodox. As a religion of sensuality (III, 653), Dionysian intoxication, and death, the Christianity of the *Hymnen* is as far from its common meaning as the historical sketch of the fifth hymn is from history— both have to be accepted as symbolic and personal accounts. Herein seems to lie the problem of a genuine appreciation of the *Hymnen*. As poems of great force and persuasion, they do demand some agreement, yet only few will be able to follow the full course of the spiritual voyage undertaken. Those who measure the cycle against the poetry of Baudelaire, Rimbaud, or Rilke will admire the bold exploration of night and death but be perhaps unwilling to accept the final Christian resolution, while those who rank it with the best Christian poetry will find the faith of the *Hymnen* idiosyncratic and perhaps even blasphemous. Standing at the great dividing line between tradition and modernity, the *Hymnen* ultimately present most readers, and for different reasons, with a question.[4]

The historical position and significance of the *Hymnen* are somewhat easier to pinpoint, because both the Christian and the Dionysian elements represented a response to enlightenment and classicism, although we must be careful not to read into their exploration of the "dark side" of life the "romantic agony" and decadence of a Marquis de Sade.

As a spiritual autobiography, the *Hymnen* encapsulate the history of a whole generation in Germany and England, which grew up in a spirit of revolt and finally reaffirmed positive religion. Thus the *Hymnen* parallel Wordsworth's poetic biography, which starts with the *Prelude* and leads to his late religious poems. Both Wordsworth and Novalis broke with stylized poetic tradition and eventually returned to stricter form. While the young Wordsworth turned to what he conceived to be the unadorned language of common people,

Novalis experimented with the personal voice of a new, irregular poetic prose; as Wordsworth's art closes with highly stylized religious sonnets, so Novalis ends his cycle with the rhymed and measured simplicity of his final hymn. Both stylistic changes reflect shifts in world views.

II   Geistliche Lieder

Novalis read some of the *Geistliche Lieder* at the November 1799 meeting of the Romantics in Jena. Unlike *Christenheit*, the *Lieder* were warmly received; Friedrich Schlegel reported to Schleiermacher that they were "the most divine" Novalis ever wrote, and their poetry was unmatched "except for the most intimate and profound early short poems of Goethe" (IV, 646). The Schlegels planned to publish the *Lieder* in the *Athenäum* under the title "Attempt at a New Spiritual Songbook" (IV, 317); however, the *Hymnen* were in the end given preference and the *Lieder* appeared only posthumously.

Novalis thought that the devotional songs of his day were usually addressed to the intellect rather than to the heart (IV, 548), and he could nowhere find that liveliness, fervor, and universality (that is, freedom from dogma) he expected from church songs (III, 588). Friedrich Klopstock's devotional songs (1758–1769) meant to be undogmatic, easily understood, and appealing to the heart, but they employed an abstract and often turgid style . Christian Fürchtegott Gellert's devotional odes and songs (1757) wanted to speak the "language of the heart," but Novalis found them wanting in stirring imagination (IV, 548). Johann Kaspar Lavater's *Christliche Lieder (Christian Songs)* (1776–1780) were still too "earthbound" because they preached morality and self-denial at the cost of mysticism and essentiality. Finally, Zinzendorf's *Teutsche Gedichte (German Poems*, 1735), which Novalis came to appreciate when he found his personal way to pietism, rejected art in favor of a simple "peasant style" and consequently often slipped into vulgarity. Novalis may have learned from their eroticism and simplicity, but he was searching for simple songs which were nevertheless "highly poetic" (III, 588).

The *Lieder* were written roughly between the summer of 1798 and September 1800. They were not intended for a unified cycle, nor is it certain that Novalis gave them their title and their order.

The earlier songs (especially I, II, IV, V, and VII) are closer to the *Hymnen* and probably contemporaneous with them, while the "Maria songs" (XIV and XV) may have been written for *Heinrich von Ofterdingen*, since they are in a manuscript that contains other songs from the novel. Between the writing of the first and the last songs, Novalis read Schleiermacher's *Über die Religion* and Jakob Boehme's writings, both of which left their mark on the *Lieder*. Schleiermacher's impact is discernible in passages of the seventh song and in the link between the *Lieder* and Novalis' planned collection of sermons or speeches (III, 588; and IV, 317): the sermons, like the songs, were to kindle an undogmatic religious enthusiasm for the sacred. Boehmean elements are evident in the mystic-pantheistic union with Christ in the twelfth song.

Since the order of the songs is accidental, we may start with the pivotal and unusual seventh, which Novalis, or the editors, entitled "Hymne." It grew out of a group of Teplitz fragments dating from the summer of 1798 that relate spiritual and bodily needs: "Is the embrace not something similar to the holy communion?" (II, 596).

Communal eating is a symbolic act of union.[. . .] All pleasure, appropriation, adaption, and assimilation is eating, or, much rather, eating is nothing but appropriation. All spiritual pleasure may therefore be represented by eating.—In a friendship one actually eats or lives off one's friends. It is a genuine trope to substitute the body for the soul, to enjoy at a memorial banquet of a friend with supernatural imagination his flesh in every bite and his blood in every drink. (II, 620)

In the "Hymne," conjugal union and religious communion become metaphoric equivalents, and the physical union of two lovers becomes the image of holy communion:

> Aber wer jemals
> Von heißen, geliebten Lippen
> Atem des Lebens sog,
> Wem heilige Glut
> In zitternde Wellen das Herz schmolz,
> Wem das Auge aufging,
> Daß er des Himmels
> Unergründliche Tiefe maß,
> Wird essen von seinem Leibe
> Und trinken von seinem Blute
> Ewiglich. (I, 167)

(But whoever has sucked from hot, beloved lips the breath of life, whose heart melted in quivering waves under holy blaze, whose eyes opened to measure the unfathomable depth of heaven, shall eat of his body and drink of his blood eternally.)

Several traditions come together in this passage. It is, of course, based on John VI:54—"he who eats my flesh and drinks my blood has eternal life"—though its eroticism is perhaps more indebted to the "Song of Songs," where the lover is often described as delicate food. Furthermore, the sensuality of these lines relies on the notion of "spiritual corporality" *(Geistleiblichkeit)* found in such mystics as Jakob Boehme, Friedrich Christoph Oetinger, and Franz von Baader. According to Oetinger, "corporality is a reality or perfection, namely if it is cleansed of the shortcomings of earthly corporality."[5] Such a cleansing is possible by partaking in the holy communion: God's incarnation through Christ has sanctified the flesh. Oetinger's sensuality may have reached Novalis through the eroticism of Zinzendorf's church songs, but Novalis' "Hymne," which Karl Barth characterized as an "absurd philosophy of the Lord's Supper" and as the clearest example of enlightened hubris,[6] intensifies pietist eroticism into an eschatological orgy:

> Einst ist alles Leib,
> *Ein* Leib,
> In himmlischem Blute
> Schwimmt das selige Paar.—
> O! daβ das Weltmeer
> Schon errötete,
> Und in duftiges Fleisch
> Aufquölle der Fels! (I, 167)

(Some day everything will be body, one body; in heavenly blood the blessed couple swims.—
O! would the world-sea yet redden, and the rock swell into fragrant flesh.)

The Maria songs (XIV and XV) represent a counterpart to the "Hymne": while the latter is written in short, unrhymed two and three stress lines which resemble the prose poetry of the first *Hymnen*, the former are in the style of the rhymed and even meter of the last *Hymnen*. Since they may have been intended as songs sung by fictional characters in *Ofterdingen*, they do not necessarily reflect Novalis' leaning toward Catholicism, though they show that he was fascinated by Catholic art and its veneration of the Madonna. Wilhelm Heinrich Wackenroder experienced a similar fascination a few years earlier, and his story of how Raphael painted his Madonna according to his inner vision rather than the features of any live woman may have been one of the inspirations for Novalis' "little Madonna song" which closes the cycle. It beautifully blends adoration with the pietistic inwardness of such expressions as *lieblich* ("lovingly") and *unnennbar süß* ("inexpressibly sweet"). The lack of imagery underscores the dissatisfaction with the Madonna's images: as in some of the other *Lieder*, the paucity of metaphors displays the rather uncatholic sentiment that art cannot convey spiritual experience:

> Ich sehe dich in tausend Bildern,
> Maria, lieblich ausgedrückt,
> Doch keins von allen kann dich schildern,
> Wie meine Seele dich erblickt.
>
> Ich weiß nur, daß der Welt Getümmel
> Seitdem mir wie ein Traum verweht,
> Und ein unnennbar süßer Himmel
> Mir ewig im Gemüte steht. (I, 177)

(I see you in thousand images / Maria, lovingly expressed, / Yet none of them can portray you / The way my soul beholds you. / I only know that the world's turmoil / Has since been blown away like a dream, / And an inexpressibly sweet heaven / Dwells in my heart forever.)

This is perhaps the most successful realization of Novalis' intent to write simple and yet highly poetic songs. The Madonna has no mediating function, and the joyful, childlike tone reflects the sheer aesthetic pleasure of beholding her with the inner eye.

In contrast, the other Maria song depicts her as the Mother and Queen of Heaven who carries the Holy Child in the fashion of Raphael's Sistine Madonna. She is addressed in unusual six line stanzas (the first five lines have four stresses, while the sixth has five) and asked for grace and protection but, characteristically, not for the absolution of sins. She is to grant that childlike disposition which the other Maria song exudes:

> Darf nur ein Kind dein Antlitz schaun,
> Und deinem Beistand fest vertraun,
> So löse doch des Alters Binde
> Und mache mich zu deinem Kinde:

Die Kindeslieb' und Kindestreu
Wohnt mir von jener goldnen Zeit noch bei. (I, 177)

(If only children are allowed to see your face, and to have confidence in
your help, then loosen the tie of my age and make me your child: childlike
love and fidelity are still with me from those golden years.)

Frequent addresses to an unconverted "thou" and occasional
shifts to the first person plural give the *Lieder* a communal dimension. Thus, in the binary structure of the opening song, the first
part portrays the speaker's escape from fear and anxiety through the
Savior, while the second recounts the redemption of a communal
"we." In the manner of Zinzendorf's pietism, redemption comes
without struggle and contrition, perhaps a touch too lightly, as Karl
Barth observed.[7] The second song, probably written for Christmas,
symbolically recounts how the fulfillment of the biblical promise
has led to a renewal of life through Christ, then admonishes a "thou"
to surrender to the Savior, and concludes again with a triumphant
communal "we." The third song recounts the deliverance from past
misery through Christ in a variant structure: the testimony of the
speaker's new life is held up to all those who still suffer as the
speaker suffered before conversion. The sixth song, which Schleiermacher reportedly recited amidst streaming tears and with trem-
bling voice,[8] addresses Christ and moves from a pledge of personal
loyalty to the final vision of a Christian community:

Wenn alle untreu werden,
So bleib' ich dir doch treu;
Da Dankbarkeit auf Erden
Nicht ausgestorben sei.
[. . .]
Einst schauen meine Brüder
Auch wieder himmelwärts,
Und sinken liebend nieder,
Und fallen dir ans Herz. (I, 165f.)

(If all become unfaithful, I'll yet remain faithful to you so that gratitude
may survive on earth [. . .] Some day my brothers will also look again
toward heaven and sink down in love and thrust themselves upon your
heart.)

In all these songs redemption is an intimately personal experience,
even though the beloved has faded into the background (she is

merely hinted at in the fourth and the thirteenth song). The universal mediators, Maria and Christ, are now pivotal to visions and redemption.

Some of the remaining songs have different themes. The eighth, for instance, is probably a *Rollengedicht* (a role poem), spoken by Maria under the cross, while the tenth and thirteenth seek consolation in Christ during physical suffering. The twelfth song is based on a Jesuit church song by the Baroque poet Friedrich von Spee. Whether Novalis knew Spee's 1628 text or a later variant is uncertain, but in any case, he must have been unaware of Spee's authorship. Spee portrays the misery of the Thirty Years War; relying on the book of Jeremiah, he pleads with the Savior to come down as rainfall and renew the valley of sorrow: "O Gott, ein Tau vom Himmel gieβ, / im Tau herab, O Heiland flieβ!" (O Lord, pour down a rain, / down the rain, oh Savior, flow!—I, 619). Novalis, who addresses most of his other songs to Christ, pleads here with the Father to release his son: "Geuβ, Vater, ihn gewaltig aus, / Gib ihn aus deinem Arm heraus" (Pour, Father, him mightily, / Release him from your arm—I, 173). Thus, Christ becomes a passive spirit that transfuses and sanctifies all parts of the world:

> In Luft und Öl, in Klang und Tau
> Durchdring' er unsrer Erde Bau.
> [. . .]
> Aus Kraut und Stein und Meer und Licht
> Schimmert sein kindlich Angesicht (I, 174)

(In air and oil, in sound, and dew / let him permeate the edifice of our earth [. . .] from herbs, and stones, and sea, and light gleams his childlike countenance.)

Since this pantheistic transfusion of nature with Christ has a Boehmean flavor, the poem was probably written after Novalis read Boehme (February 1800). The Boehmean Christian renewal is metaphorically also a return to a golden age and to childhood:

> Der Winter weicht, ein neues Jahr
> Steht an der Krippe Hochaltar.
> Es ist das erste Jahr der Welt.
> Die sich dies Kind erst selbst bestellt. (I, 174)

(Winter gives way, a new year / waits at the manger's high altar. / It is the first year of the world / Which this child will bring about by itself.)

Appropriately, the song on the Christ Child is followed by one where the beloved reappears and by the two final ones addressed to Maria.

With the exception of the "Hymne," the *Lieder* are formally closer to the metric and verbal simplicity of the last *Hymnen* than to the unusual rhythm and imagery of the first ones. Keeping in the tradition of the church songs, these poems show an all but uniform alternation of stressed and unstressed syllables—a feature much less common in German than in English and the Romance languages, because in German the unstressed syllables carry little weight and their number between stressed syllables may vary considerably. Eight of the fourteen songs have simple four stress lines, the sixth and the tenth have three stresses, the fifth and the ninth alternate between three and four stress lines, while the second and the fourteenth use four stresses but switch to five stresses in the last two and the first lines respectively.

Only six of the songs have four line stanzas, five of them are in unusual six line stanzas, while three of them contain eight line stanzas. Alternating masculine and feminine cross-rhymes are the rule, except in the twelfth song, which follows the original by using masculine couplets, and in the songs with six line stanzas. The latter are structured as follows: the fourth and the eighth have two feminine couplets separated by masculine rhymes in the third and sixth line (aabccd), the second has feminine and masculine cross-rhymes followed by a feminine couplet (ababcc), while the fourteenth has two masculine couplets separated by a feminine one (aabbcc). The unusual metric sophistication of the fifth song, which may account for its twenty-odd musical settings (among them one by Schubert), may best be appreciated by a quick look at its first stanza:

> Wenn ich ihn nur habe,
> Wenn er mein nur ist,
> Wenn mein Herz bis hin zum Grabe
> Seine Treue nie vergiβt:
> Weiβ ich nichts von Leide,
> Fühle nichts, als Andacht, Lieb' und Freude. (I, 164)

(If only I have him / if only he is mine / If my heart until the grave / its loyalty never forgets: / I shall know nothing of suffering, / feel nothing but devotion, love, and joy.)

This formally most intricate song fuses thought and expression. As in the second song, feminine and masculine cross-rhymes are followed by a feminine couplet, but the fluctuating stress pattern of the lines (3,3,4,4,3,5) creates a second cohesive structure, so that the ebb and flow of unequal lines interlaces with the rhyme, creating a poignant sensation of expectation and hesitancy which reflects the speaker's state of mind. The if-when pattern of the first stanza is repeated in the next three, indicating that the peace in Christ is not yet achieved, but is yearned for and enjoyed in anticipation. In church songs, repetitive and strict rhythm lends assurance and security to the singers, while here the fluctuating rhythm reflects the speaker's timid joy and his fear that he may not be able to fully attain bliss.

Due to their indebtedness to the church song tradition and their intended broader audience, the songs are as limited in their vocabulary, style, and themes as in their metric patterns. Instead of the materiality of the world, they portray the fluctuations of mood, emotion, and attitude between depravity and blessedness. The spiritual oscillation is described in fairly standard formal structures and with a narrow range of recurrent vocabulary. Excepting the "Hymne" and the twelfth, originally Catholic, song, the simplicity of language and the absence of objects severely limit the use of metaphors. The dominating subject, *Herz* (heart), repeatedly experiences joy, sorrow, love, and weeping; the state of blessedness is "sweet pain," "sweet refreshment," "sweet heaven," while the other moods and emotions have a similar pietistic gentleness to them. Maria is loved *herzensinniglich* (the untranslatable term means something like "with heart-felt intimacy"), but even unrepentent sinners are "quivering captives" (*bebende Gefangene*).

The typical sentence is simple, short, and without inversions, except in the thirteenth song, where the contrasting moods of dejection and consolation are each represented by a carefully constructed elaborate single sentence: the "when" clause of the first eight line stanza is followed by a "then" clause in the second. I give the complete text:

> Wenn in bangen trüben Stunden
> Unser Herz beinah verzagt,
> Wenn von Krankheit überwunden

Angst in unserm Innern nagt;
Wir der Treugeliebten denken,
Wie sie Gram und Kummer drückt,
Wolken unsern Blick beschränken,
Die kein Hoffnungsstrahl durchblickt:

O! dann neigt sich Gott herüber,
Seine Liebe kommt uns nah,
Sehnen wir uns dann hinüber,
Steht sein Engel vor uns da,
Bringt den Kelch des frischen Lebens,
Lispelt Mut und Trost uns zu;
Und wir beten nicht vergebens
Auch für die Geliebten Ruh. (I, 175)

(When in fearful gloomy hours / Our heart almost desponds, / When overwhelmed by disease / Fear gnaws inside; / we think of the faithfully loved ones, / How they are burdened with affliction and sorrow, / Clouds obstruct our vision, / Which no ray of hope pierces:

Oh, then God leans over to us, / his love approaches us, / If then we yearn to be yonder, / His angel stands in front of us, / Brings the chalice of fresh life, / Whispers courage and consolation to us; / And we do not pray vainly / For the peace of our loved ones.)

The *Geistliche Lieder* minimize artfulness and strive to express a religious sentiment that moves within tradition without being dogmatic. Because of their simplicity, they became Novalis' most popular poems, but for this reason, they are seldom appreciated aesthetically and often not even identified as poems by Novalis. According to one anecdote, Novalis' father once sang in church the first song and, unaware of the author, was deeply touched by it (I, 124f.). Several of the songs (especially the first, fifth, sixth, and ninth) were adopted by nineteenth-century Protestant and Catholic songbooks, though occasionally they had to be adjusted to fit the dogma. Dilthey was probably right in remarking that they will live on with Christianity.[9]

III *Last Poems*

Apart from the *Hymnen* and the *Lieder*, Novalis' late poetry includes the songs in *Heinrich von Ofterdingen*, which I shall discuss in the next chapter; a few occasional poems, which will be included in my account of Novalis' last years; and a few quite new and unusual poems. I shall now single out three of the latter to indicate the new directions: "Der Himmel war umzogen" ("The Skies were Covered"), "Alle Menschen seh ich leben" ("All People I see Living"), and "Das Gedicht" ("The Poem").

In "Der Himmel," the intimations of Novalis' personal life in the spring of 1800 are woven into a charming mythic episode, narrated in the style of a folksong. Under a cloudy sky, the dejected speaker dreams of flying away with his beloved to a place of eternal spring; he receives a wand from a child, touches with it the "queen of the snakes" that slithers in the nearby bushes, and gains immeasurable riches. The poem may have been occasioned by Novalis' engagement to Julie and his desire to get money for the marriage (in which case the enriching snake could be a Sophie figure), but it is symbolic rather than allegorical, allowing for a mythic interpretation with no reference to biography. The magic wand and the snake (symbol of rejuvenation and spender of wealth), as well as the simple three stress lines with cross-rhymes are hallmarks of folk poetry.

"Alle Menschen," perhaps Novalis' last poem (late autumn 1800), represents a contrast because it is meditative, confessional, and intellectual rather than narrative, symbolic, and folksonglike. "All people" are divided into the "foolish many" who lightly levitate in pleasure and the "wise few" that laboriously struggle to reach a "higher" rest. The final stanza seems to affirm active life:

> Ruh ist Göttern nur gegeben
> Ihnen ziemt der Überfluβ
> Doch für uns ist Handeln Leben
> Macht zu üben nur Genuβ. (I, 420)

(Rest is only given to gods / overabundance is their domain / But for us action is life / The exercise of power the only pleasure.)[10]

This conclusion is put in question, however, by a reference to a "single one" in the first stanza, who achieves a "light striving, levitating life"—that is, a reconciliation of rest and striving. Whether man can achieve this or only a god is not clear, but a diary entry from September 6, 1800, suggests the former: "Rest is the true state of man. For the peaceful man every external situation is bearable and even pleasant. One doesn't sense the fatal striving, and even boredom is easy to take. To the quiet person everything is easy and comfortable. All representations, all thoughts of religion become vigorous and uplifting, and the truly heavenly joy of activity awakens forcefully" (IV, 57). Perhaps the poem affirms in a similar way both active and contemplative lives and rejects only that state of rest which wastes itself in shallow pleasure. Its form indeed reflects a balance between rest and unrest, regularity and irregularity: even rhythm and careful construction encompass changing rhymes, irregular stanzas, and an unusually differentiated vocabulary.

"Das Gedicht" seems to have gone furthest toward abstract symbolism, for its images do not point toward anything but are held together and given meaning by the structure into which they are fitted. The lyric self is neither apparent nor referred to. Language seems to liberate itself from world and mind, things and ideas. Structurally, the eight stanza poem falls into two equal parts separated by the shift from present to past tense in the middle. The first part suggests the interior of a church with high, solid arches; a sacred object reminds of a holy past when the spirit resided on earth, while a "lost page" presages a revival of it:

> Unter hohen festen Bogen
> Nur von Lampenlicht erhellt
> Liegt, seitdem der Geist entflogen
> Nun das Heiligste der Welt.
>
> Leise kündet bessre Tage
> Ein verlornes Blatt uns an
> Und wir sehn der alten Sage
> Mächtige Augen aufgetan. (I, 410)

(Under high, solid arches / Brightened by the light of a lamp only / Has been lying, since the spirit flew away, / The Holiest of the world.

A lost page quietly announces better days to us / And we see the ancient legend's powerful eyes opened.)

The second part of the poem seems to plunge into that mythic past, describing a festival which culminates in the brief appearance of the "flower queen":

> Liebe brachte gefüllte Becher
> Also perlt in Blumen der Geist
> Ewig trinken die kindlichen Zecher

Bis der geheiligte Teppich zerreißt.
[. . .]
Endlich von farbigen Käfern getragen
Kam die Blumenfürstin allein.

Schleier, wie Wolken zogen
Von der blendenden Stirn zu den FüBen
Wir fielen nieder sie zu grüBen—
Wir weinten bald—sie war entflogen. (I, 410)

(Love brought filled chalices / Thus sparkles spirit in flowers / Eternally drink the childlike tipplers / Until the blessed rug tears. [. . .] Finally, carried by colored beatles / Came the flower queen alone.

Veils, like clouds, passed from her resplendent forehead to her feet / We fell down to greet her— / We soon wept—she was gone.)

The language of the poem is kept so vague that instead of a concrete single meaning, many different ones can be construed. Only the temporal structure is clear: within a triadic mythic history, the past is kept alive by the memory of the flower queen and the future is poetically anticipated. As in the poetry of Hölderlin, poet and poem seem to be earthly representatives of the divine in those transitory times when the gods are hidden.

IV *Theory of Poetry*

We may divide Novalis' mature poetry into three general categories, each of which is explored in his theoretical statements: (1) the prose poetry of the early *Hymnen*, (2) the simple religious poetry of the later *Hymnen* and most of the *Lieder*, and (3) some of the latest poems tending toward abstract symbolism.

Although the immediate reasons for the new form are not known, the prose poetry of the first *Hymnen* may be regarded as part of a larger effort to fuse poetry and prose in the spirit of Schlegel's *Universalpoesie*. Well before turning the verses into prose, Novalis had already considered the demands of prose poetry, though he came to conclusions he did not carry out. On January 12, 1798, he suggested to August Wilhelm Schlegel that prose poetry's looser organization and meter should be tied to a "more transparent and colorless expression." He did not adopt such an expression in the first *Hymnen*, perhaps because these prose poems were more object-oriented than the verse sections and therefore in need of more colorful expression.

"Transparent and colorless expression"—that is, a language that does not call attention to itself, is more typical of the second category, the *Lieder* and later *Hymnen*, because their sphere is further removed from the world into an interior space which has no physical equivalents: "I see you in thousand images, yet none of them can portray the way my soul beholds you" (I, 177). Most of these verses do not contain images but merely feelings, moods, and beliefs and their shifts (*Gemütsbewegung*) from dejection to hope, from loneliness to faith. Since this poetry wishes to elicit corresponding shifts in the reader, it also functions as *Gemütserregungskunst*, an art that stimulates the spirit. The *Hymnen* and *Lieder* should mediate religious experience to the reader. The poet assumes the roles of prophets and priests and becomes a leader of mankind: "Poets and priests were one at the beginning, and only later ages have separated them. But the true poet always remained a priest, just as the true priest always remained a poet. And shouldn't the future reestablish the old state of affairs?" (II, 441). However, if poetry becomes enigmatic, as in Novalis' last poems, universal symbols become private, and language acquires a plurality of meaning. The thoughts and feelings excited in the reader no longer need to correspond to those experienced by the poet, as reading becomes a second creation. This third category, that of abstract poetry, divides into two: in the first the poet is in complete control of his material, in the second the formative force is the universal structure of the mind embodied in language.

The first of the two abstract modes is theoretically supported by an extension of idealism. In obvious reference to Kant, Novalis notes in the "Brouillon": "The poetic philosopher is in the position of an absolute creator. Even the circle, a triangle are created this way. Nothing is added to them except of what their producer allows to be added" (III, 415). This relies on Kant's notion that mathematical representations are "constructed" out of certain mental entities—namely, concepts. In poetry, these entities may also be emotions or changes in mood, in which case poetry becomes musical. Novalis' poetry is expressive primarily through its musical qualities: rhythm and meter overshadow metaphor and imagery; verbs, fortified by expressive adverbs, register states and changes of in-

wardness; nouns and adjectives are generally pale. This musicality
of Novalis' language is the prime vehicle of his "auditory" eroticism,
which portrays desire, lust, and yearning rather than the visual
quality of objects responsible for them.

The tendency toward music suggests a nonrepresentative, logically incoherent poetic language: "Poems—merely sonorous and full
of beautiful words—but also without sense and coherence—at most
individual stanzas understandable—they must be like fragments
from the most divergent things" (III, 572). Poetic words are, then,
abstract musical notes which acquire meaning from the composition,
the particular way in which the acoustic patterns of language are
shaped into a poetic meaning. Novalis follows the eighteenth-century tradition which regained prominence with the linguistics of
Saussure and contemporary semiotics, believing that linquistic signs
are conventions which have no intrinsic relation to their referent.
He goes beyond this view by envisioning and experimenting with
a poetry which breaks convention, anticipating thereby the Symbolist theory and practice of Verlaine, Rimbaud, Mallarmé, Valéry,
Hofmannsthal, Trakl, and others.

This new conception of poetry intends to reduce the semantic
units of language (words) to the role of meaningless phonological
units. The resultant poetic constructs are also like algebraic formulas
containing arbitrarily chosen letters: algebraic letters perform certain functions and may acquire concrete meaning, just as concrete
nouns, verbs, adjectives, and other parts of speech may be fitted
into a syntactic structure. This "structuralist" conception of poetic
language is the second version of Novalis' theory of abstract poetry.
Conceiving of syntax as a general rule for combining the parts of
speech and of language as a combinatorics of words, Novalis adopted
the Leibnizian ideas on symbolic logic and combinatorial mathematics. Transposing them into poetry he came to think of poetic
language as an abstract and general syntactic structure which imposed itself upon the poet's mind and subordinated semantic content
to structural context. Poems could thus emerge not from ideas or
words but from a "musical" sentence or phrase structure into which
specific parts of speech would be "plugged" according to the demands of rhythm, sonority, and imagery—a method which Georg
Trakl seems to have actually followed.[11] The first part of the following *Monolog* is the key document of this view of poetic language,

while the second part attempts to reconcile the dominance of the abstract and transindividual structure with the possibility of individual expression.

V   *Monolog*

Speaking and writing are actually odd matters; true talk is mere word play. One cannot but be astonished by the ridiculous, mistaken belief that we are talking for the sake of objects. Nobody seems to understand that language is unique because it cares only about itself. That's why she is such a wonderful and fertile secret—when one speaks just for the sake of speaking, one utters the most magnificent and original truths. But if one wishes to speak about something definite, moody language makes one say the most ridiculous and twisted things. That is also the source of the hatred which so many serious people feel against language. They notice her playfulness, do not notice however that her scorned chatter is the infinitely serious side of language. If one could only explain to people that language behaves like mathematical formulas—they form a world of their own, they play only with themselves, express nothing but their own wonderful nature, and for this very reason they are expressive, just because of this they mirror the strange interplay of objects. Only through their freedom are they members of nature, and only in their free movements does the world soul express itself and turn them into a gentle measure and blueprint of things. So it is with language: whoever inwardly registers the gentle effects of its inner nature and moves his tongue or his hands accordingly is going to be a prophet; while those who know well but have inadequate ears or sense to write truths like these will be fooled by language and ridiculed by people, just as Cassandra was by the Trojans. While I believe I have defined thereby most clearly the essence and function of poetry, I also know that nobody will understand it and no poetry is made that way. But what if I had to speak? And what if this drive to speak would be the sign of language inspiration, the activity of language in me? And what if my willpower would want to do everything I had to do?—then, in the end, without my knowing and believing, this could become poetry and make a secret of language comprehensible. Wouldn't I then be a writer by calling, since a writer is, after all, just somebody who is possessed by language? (II, 672f.)

According to this line in Novalis' poetics, language is a set of internalized rules in the mind capable of generating texts without rational control and guidance. Language imposes itself upon the speaker; the poet is not a divine creator but merely a powerless medium in which language articulates itself. Novalis' conception is related to surrealist notions on "automatic writing" and to T. S.

Eliot's idea that the poet is a mere catalyst because according to all three theories the poet has no control over language. But in "automatic writing," that control is relinquished to the subconscious; in Eliot, to experience and tradition, and in Novalis, to the sovereign power of language itself. The ability of language to generate texts according to its syntactic and combinatorial rules was a notion that also fascinated Heinrich von Kleist, who wrote a remarkable essay *Über die all mähliche Verfertigung der Gedanken beim Reden (On the Gradual Formation of Thought in the Course of Speaking)*, claiming that meaning comes in the process of speaking and that problems often get solved by surrendering intellectual control to the act of speaking. In this view, poetic language is neither a mirror to nature nor a lamp radiating from the mind of a genius, but a set of rules whose application generates texts. In everyday language, these rules are used to allow communication and to achieve specific purposes; but poetic language serves its own end; it is, in Kant's sense, "purposive without [any specific] purpose."[12] In this, Novalis anticipates important modes of modern poetry, although he is building on tenets of an idealism which most modern poets no longer hold. For Novalis, the formulaic structure of poetry is pivotal because here, freed from the service of everyday communication, language reveals the universal structure of the mind, a structure which he considers to exist in some kind of "preestablished harmony" with the structure of the universe. The more language is liberated, the more readily it will reveal the world. Free language plays "only with itself," but, doing so, it mirrors the "strange interplay of objects."

CHAPTER 7

The Novelist: Heinrich von Ofterdingen

I *The Struggle with Goethe's* Wilhelm Meister

O N February 27, 1799, Novalis conveyed to Caroline Schlegel his mixed reactions to Friedrich's novel *Lucinde* and added that his own would be totally different: "I am inclined to devote my whole life to a single novel which should constitute a whole library by itself and perhaps portray the apprenticeship of a whole nation. The word 'apprenticeship' is incorrect, it expresses a specific direction. For me it means nothing but years of transition from the infinite to the finite" (IV, 281). Although it is not certain that these remarks pertain to *Ofterdingen*, they touch upon two of its central features: the encyclopedic size, which links it to the "Brouillon," and the notion of "apprenticeship," which leads us, once more, to Goethe's novel.

Novalis wrote the plan and the first sections of his novel in the township of Artern, where he inspected the salt works and found, in the library of a friend, Johannes Rothe's fifteenth-century chronicle about the legendary medieval *Minnesänger* Heinrich von Afterdingen, a poet who reputedly participated in the famous Wartburg song contest. Novalis proceeded well with the writing, but the project kept growing: in January 1800, he thought he could finish by Easter (IV, 318); by February 23 he thought he had completed about twelve printed sheets, but was already planning two volumes. He completed the first one by April 5, while the second remained unfinished.

Novalis' February 1800 letter to Tieck, which gratefully acknowledged Tieck's suggestion to read Jakob Boehme, contains some

126

further indication of the forces that shaped *Ofterdingen*. Boehme changed Novalis' view of his *Lehrlinge* and became an inspiration for *Ofterdingen*, which was now planned as an "apotheosis of poetry," with Heinrich's initiation in the first part and his transfiguration in the second. As a novel of a young artist, *Ofterdingen* was to bear some resemblance to Tieck's *Franz Sternbalds Wanderungen*, without achieving its levity: "This is, in every respect, a first attempt, the first fruit of that poetry which reawakened in me and to whose resurgence your friendship contributed most. Among speculative minds I have almost become pure speculation" (IV, 322). In the continuation of his letter to Tieck, Novalis vehemently attacked *Wilhelm Meister:*

Much as I have learned and still do from *Meister,* the whole book is fundamentally odious to me. [. . .] It is a Candide against poetry, a novel to which the title of nobility has been conferred. One doesn't know who comes off worse, poetry or the nobility—poetry because it is attributed to the nobility or nobility because it is associated with poetry. Its garden of poetry is feigned with straw and rags. Instead of turning the comediennes into muses, the muses are made into comediennes. It is incomprehensible to me how I could be blind so long. The intellect is like a naive devil in the book. (IV, 323)

Notebook entries, which Novalis planned to incorporate in a critical article, complete the negative perspective on Goethe's novel:

Wilhelm Meisters Lehrjahre is so to speak thoroughly prosaic—and modern. The romantic sinks to ruin in it—the poetry of nature, the miraculous as well. It treats merely everyday human things—nature and mysticism are altogether forgotten. It is a poeticized bourgeois and domestic story. The miraculous is expressly treated in it as poetry and wild enthusiasm. Artistic atheism is the spirit of the book. Very much economy—the poetic effect is achieved with prosaic, cheap material. (III, 638f.)
Wilhelm Meisters Lehrjahre, or the pilgrimage to obtain the patent of nobility. (III, 646)

The target of the attack seems evident: Goethe followed Meister's vagaries in the theater but finally turned him into a country squire, which seemed like a travesty of the poetic and religious views Novalis held.

These attacks are in sharp contrast to Novalis' earlier opinions of

Meister. He had read it for the first time immediately after its publication and had planned to co-author with Friedrich Schlegel a review of it. He returned to it after Sophie's death, and notebook entries suggest that the life-affirming tone of Goethe's novel and its concern with the business of life may have helped Novalis to overcome his spiritual crisis and "sickness unto death." Schlegel's great essay on *Meister*, published in July 1798 in the *Athenäum*, rekindled Novalis' interest once more and led him to praise Goethe as a scientist and poet, albeit with dubious compliments which foreshadow the later attacks:

Goethe is an altogether practical poet. He is in his works what the English are in their wares—extremely simple, attractive, comfortable, and durable. He has done for German literature what Wedgwood did for the English art world—he has, like the English, an intellectually acquired refined taste with an innate economy. [. . .] In scope, richness, and depth he is surpassed here and there, but who would dare to compare himself to him in didactic art? [. . .] The seat of [his] actual art lies merely in his intellect, which creates according to a concept unique to it. Merely fantasy, wit, and judgment are required of it. Thus *Wilhelm Meister* is fully an art product, a work of the intellect. [. . .] Goethe will and must be surpassed—but only the way the ancients are surpassable: in content and force, in richness and depth. Not actually as an artist, or at least only to a very small degree, for his soundness and austerity are perhaps already more exemplary than it appears. (II, 640–42)

Novalis took up the challenge of surpassing Goethe by carefully planning his *Ofterdingen* as a counterpart to *Meister*, to the point of wanting to publish it with the same publisher and in the same format. Against *Meister*'s contemporary setting, he chose a medieval milieu which eventually was to lead into myth and fairytale: "The closing is a transition from the real world into the secret one— death—last dream and awakening. Here the supernatural, the fairy-tale like must already shimmer through everywhere" (I, 342).

Yet this neat and sharp contrast to Goethe's *Meister* doesn't tell the whole story. By the time that Novalis assumed administrative responsibilities, he became much better disposed toward the spirit of mercantilism than *Glauben und Liebe* would lead us to believe. Already in *Blütenstaub* he had praised the "true merchant spirit" of the Medici and Fuggers against the "petty shopkeepers" of his age (II, 439). In the "Brouillon" he went further and accepted the trade spirit as the "spirit of the world": "It sets everything in motion and ties everything together. It awakens countries and cities, nations and works of art. It is the spirit of culture—of mankind's perfection" (III, 464). Far from condemning the mercantile spirit in *Ofterdingen*, Novalis sends off his Heinrich in the company of cultured merchants who are connoisseurs and storytellers. While they provide the lowest stage of the young poet's education, they make an important and positive contribution to it. Furthermore, Novalis carried out the assault on the poetic and moral principles of *Meister* largely with techniques borrowed from it: the notes for *Ofterdingen* clearly demonstrate that he developed his compositional ideas from those combinatorial and serial principles in mathematics which he believed to form the structural basis of Goethe's *Meister*. The most important of these was the "variational principle," to regard all figures of the novel as reflections of, and variations on, a single individual.

Novalis and Schlegel believed that variation established a network of associations within Goethe's novel, a set of secret affinities which showed that such figures as Natalie and the "beautiful soul" (the authoress of a fictional diary in *Meister*) were "the same individual in variations" (II, 561). Subsequently, Novalis extended this principle to all of Goethe's major figures: "Lothario is but the manly Therese with a transition to Meister. Natalie—the combination and ennoblement of the aunt and Therese" (III, 312). This variational principle was no mere novelistic technique but, so Novalis believed, an artistic mirror of a Leibnizian universe: "All men are variations of a single complete individual, i.e., of a marriage. [. . .] If a simple variation such as Natalie and the beautiful soul already awakens such deep pleasure, how infinite must the pleasure be of somebody who registers the whole in its powerful symphony?" (II, 564). Accordingly, Novalis established a similar network of affinities and secret identities among the teacher figures of *Ofterdingen*, and he suggested that the characters of the novel and the figures from the inserted tales would reveal their interrelation in the second part (I, 342). The most important of these affinities links Mathilde, Heinrich's beloved, and Cyane, a girl Heinrich encounters after Mathilde's death in the second part.

While Novalis read into Goethe's novel this structure of characterization, his method and his world view differed from Goethe's, and in fact, he misjudged the role of intellect in the organization of *Wilhelm Meister*. Goethe strove for individualization, and although he may have consciously applied variation to delicately suggest the unity underlying variety, he was reluctant to use schemes to establish a philosophical perspective. When Schiller urged him to do so, Goethe replied on July 9, 1796: "No doubt, the apparent results that I state are much more limited than the content of the work, and I appear to myself like one who, after having piled many large numbers on top of each other, has finally made a deliberate error in the addition to reduce the final sum out of God knows what caprice."[1] Goethe's failure to "add up" his novel is as symptomatic of his method as Novalis' use of mathematical vocabulary to describe his. Novalis believed that the human variety can be ordered mathematically, because he perceived human beings as members of an "ascending and descending line from the infinitely small to the infinitely large" (III, 429). His novel was to order this infinite variety by utilizing principles of variation and by placing the interrelated figures within the novel's "geometric progression" (II, 534). Thus, Novalis agrees with Goethe that the idea of a novel is verbally inexpressible, but he finds a mathematical series appropriate to it: "The novel is an intuitive execution, the realization of an idea. But an idea cannot be captured in a sentence. An idea is an infinite series of sentences—an irrational quantity, not to be set musically, incommensurate. [. . .] However, the law of its progression can be established, and by this principle should a novel be criticized" (II, 570). Novalis thought that the figures of *Meister* could be ordered in a series (II, 647), but he ultimately criticized that principle of progression because it led in an inappropriate direction.

II *Narrative Structure and Perspective*

The setting of *Ofterdingen* is medieval Germany, but the novel cannot be called historical because it is short on those descriptive passages and characterizations which establish a historical atmosphere. The first part, entitled "Die Erwartung" ("The Expectation"), traces the journey of young Heinrich and his mother from Eisenach in Thuringia, where his father is an artisan, to the rich commercial city of Augsburg, where Heinrich's maternal grandfather, Schwaning, lives a more mundane and carefree life. The visitors arrive amidst a festivity and mingle with the guests, which include the poet Klingsohr and his daughter Mathilde. Heinrich and Mathilde instantly fall in love. Heinrich's subsequent dream foreshadows Mathilde's death, but next morning his poetic love and his love for poetry are still in happy harmony: Klingsohr acquaints him with the principles of poetry, and his engagement to Mathilde becomes official.

The very possibility of such a capsule summary indicates that plot is not an asset in Novalis' craft of fiction. The threadbare story lacks suspenseful action and receives no enrichment from diverting subplots in the fashion of eighteenth-century novels (including *Meister*). The role of secondary plots is assumed by Klingsohr's tale and by two shorter fictional inserts, the stories of Arion (I, 211–13) and Atlantis (I, 213–29). These three narrative inserts, which take up more than a third of the novel, are obliquely integrated into the main plot through a network of affinities and mirror effects, according to the technique developed by Goethe in his *Unterhaltungen deutscher Ausgewanderten* (*Conversations among German Emigrants*, 1794) and in *Meister*, where the extraneous "Tagebuch einer schönen Seele" ("Diary of a Beautiful Soul") is a comparable fictional insert.

In *Ofterdingen*, the combinatorial techniques are applied not only to the characters and the inserted stories, but also to the different genres, styles, and modes of discourse as defined by Friedrich Schlegel. The aim and mission of his "progressive universal poetry" was

now to mingle, now to fuse poetry and prose, genius and criticism, the poetry of the educated and the poetry of the people, to make life and society poetic, to poeticize wit, to fill and saturate the forms of art with matters of genuine cultural value and to quicken them with the vibrations of humor. It embraces everything that is poetic, from the most comprehensive system of art [. . .] to the sigh or kiss which the poetic child expresses in artless song.[2]

Schlegel's notion was indeed a blueprint for an encyclopedic novel which was attempted in *Ofterdingen* and further developed by such twentieth-century novelists as Thomas Mann.[3] Schlegel's conception of the novel illuminates, furthermore, that Novalis' "Brouillon" and *Ofterdingen* were interlinked by the common attempt to unite through combinatorial principles a vast array of conceptual and formal elements: if the encyclopedia concentrated on ideas, the novel was to become encyclopedic both in ideas and forms of discourse.

Following Goethe and Tieck, Novalis interspersed his narrative with thirteen poems and three stories, and he made such heavy use of dramatic dialogues that the plot actually boils down to a sequence of conversations which gradually widen Heinrich's horizon and raise his consciousness. Not visual travel impressions, but a series of intellectual and emotional events is the staple of his education; the novel presents static situations which give rise to conversations, inner monologues, and stories. The range of conversational topics makes *Ofterdingen* an idea encyclopedia in which the entries are arranged along the lines of Heinrich's development, each of them closing not with a logical conclusion but with a poetic statement contained in a tale, a poem, or a dream.

Let us briefly follow the conversational "plot" of *Ofterdingen*. The first chapter takes place in Eisenach before the departure, the following four chronicle the journey, while the last four take place in Augsburg. The opening conversation between Heinrich and his parents about dreams ends with the father's recollection that a dream led to his marriage. The journey divides into three phases. First, conversations with accompanying merchants lead to a consideration of poetry in life and end with the legend of Arion and the tale of Atlantis, narrated by the merchants. The second stage is set in an unnamed castle, where the travelers spend the night and Heinrich has two contrasting encounters: first he is among knights who prepare for a crusade in a blustering and bloodthirsty mood; then he talks to Zulima, a young Saracen captive, who provides a counterperspective by revealing to him the measure of suffering resulting from war. In the final stage of the journey, Heinrich encounters two memorable "underground" figures: the old miner, who tells him about the pleasure of discovering the treasures of the earth, and the hermit, who initiates him into the life of contemplation, the mysteries of scripture, and the significance of history. In the words of Klingsohr: "The land of poetry, the romantic East, greeted you with its sweet melancholy; war addressed you in its wild magnificence, and nature and history came across your path in the figure of a miner and a hermit" (I, 283).

The Augsburg conversations between Klingsohr and Heinrich about poetry and love take up the seventh chapter and part of the eighth, leading to the engagement of Heinrich and Mathilde. Klingsohr's tale closes the first part of the novel. The conversational partners fall therefore into two categories: they are representatives of social groups (parents, merchants, knights, slaves, guests at Schwaning's house) or they are teachers (the miner, the hermit, Klingsohr). Heinrich's love for Mathilde introduces him both to a teacher, Klingsohr, and to the social institution of the family.

The dominant role of conversations in the novel has hitherto unappreciated effects on its narrative style. The predominance of speech is a corollary to sparse portrayal and lack of individualized character description. The merchants have no names, and their remarks are often attributed to the group as a whole; the knights, the residents along the journey, and the guests at Schwaning's festivity are identified only as members of a group. Even the identity of the central characters is established by their utterances rather than by their appearances or behavior: the miner, the hermit, Zulima, Klingsohr, Mathilde, or Heinrich's father come to life in their reminiscences, their praise of their profession, or simply in the quality of their language. Their external appearance is briefly described with a limited vocabulary and rough distinctions. The economy in characterization goes hand in hand with a disinterest in the environment. Eisenach and Augsburg, the departure and terminal points of the journey, remain mere dots on the map without physical presence; the stages of the journey are denoted with such Shakespearean labels as "a village," "a castle," "a cave," and the individual scenes are given a setting only inasmuch as they affect the mind of the protagonist. Obviously, the historical milieu is not a vehicle to evoke the life and manners of a bygone age, but a means to alienate the reader from his own world and to sharpen his imagination through a transposition of everyday events into an unknown sphere.

The opening of the novel illustrates some of these features and suggests further characteristics of Novalis' narrative style:

The parents were already in bed and slept, the clock struck with monotonous beat, in front of the clattering window whistled the wind; intermittently, the chamber was brightened by the shimmer of the moon. The youth lay restlessly on his bed and remembered the stranger and his stories. "Not the treasures awakened in me such an unspeakable desire," he said to himself, "far from me lies all greed: but I yearn to behold the blue flower." (I, 195)

This introduction gives no information about the time and the place of the action, and it identifies people only generically, as parents,

youth, and stranger. Furthermore, the narrator has little concern
for the substantiality of objects because he characterizes them only
by the motions they perform, the sounds they make, or the light
that is shed upon them and not by the visual or tactile qualities that
make them palpable: the clock beats, the window clatters, the wind
whistles, the moonlight and the (unmentioned) clouds perform a
dance of light upon the walls. Excepting the parents, nothing is at
rest, everything partakes of an eery performance of "sight and
sound" that dissolves the objects into simultaneous temporal movements. As Novalis remarked, space is the precipitation of time (III,
564); time flowing, variable space (III, 427f.; see also III, 65 and
455). This temporalization of the world holds for the novel at large:
the movement from Eisenach to Augsburg is temporal rather than
spatial because of the deliberate inattention to the spatial world
and, even more so, due to an expansion of the temporal dimension.
The latter is achieved by a variety of means, of which the transfer-
ence of the action into a distant past is only the first and perhaps
least important example. The dreams, which recollect, but point
toward the future; the discovery of a prophetic book in the hermit's
cave; the reminiscences of the father, Zulima, the miner, and the
hermit; and, ultimately, the narrative inserts all lie beyond the
temporal terminals of the journey. Dreams and reminiscenses have
a primary role in endowing the simple plot with a complex temporal
structure; they interfuse the present with the past and future and
engender Heinrich's peculiar sensation that everything is pregnant
with prophecy and laden with the memory of dimly felt past events
buried in his subconscious. Heinrich moves within that single con-
tinuum of space-time which Novalis envisaged, but, as for instance
in the first mention of the blue flower, he experiences objects as
temporal relations. Heinrich (just like Hyazinth) recalls a stranger's
visit and remembers his account of a flower, the attainment of which
will be the distant goal of this life.

The temporal movements of the opening scene have different
rhythms: the even measure of the parents' sleep and the monotony
of the clock contrast with the rattle, the play of the moonlight, and
Heinrich's restless tossing. But the rapid convergence toward the
preoccupations of the youth indicates that the movements in the
world merely provide parallels with and contrasts to psychic changes
in the protagonist.[4] This typical feature of the novel suggests that
Novalis' narrative perspective is different from Goethe's. In *Meister*,

an omniscient narrator rules over the ample epic world of his own creation, while in *Ofterdingen,* the narrator identifies with his protagonist. Except for two longer authorial intrusions at the opening of Chapters II and VI,[5] the narrated world is seen from Heinrich's confining perspective, and nothing is registered that could not be seen, heard, or felt by him: the narrator's perspective coincides with Heinrich's. This has important consequences. First, it restricts the narrator's spatial overview; second, it excludes him from the minds of his other characters. Since these figures and their motivation are understandable only inasmuch as they are comprehensible to Heinrich, whose psychological insights are as yet unsophisticated, the readers are presented with a phenomenological portrayal of the characters and their interaction. They see events with the eyes of a passive protagonist, who registers every new impression with surprise and merely a dim sense of their interrelation. Nor does the narrative concentration on Heinrich yield insights into his psyche, for we know him only inasmuch as he knows himself, and he is as yet too inexperienced to articulate his introspection. The restricted narrative perspective allows Novalis to create a sense of mystery.

Readers familiar with the works of Kafka will recognize that Novalis' narrative technique anticipates that of *The Trial* and *The Castle.* Neither author integrates or complements the protagonist's perceptions. But while Kafka aims at a sense of confusion, alienation, and disorientation, Novalis intends to sharpen the readers' sensitivity to intimations from another world which remain imperceptible amidst the humdrum of everyday. When Kafka replaces description, plot, and character portrayal by conversations, he exposes his protagonists to hostility and destructive information, while Heinrich encounters benevolent people who contribute to his education each in their own way. The conversations in *Ofterdingen,* therefore, satisfy Schlegel's dictum that novels are modern Socratic dialogues,[6] while those of Kafka do not. The same technique serves different artistic and philosophical purposes.

In two important respects, the reader is not restricted to Heinrich's consciousness. Though the narrator observes things from Heinrich's perspective and refrains from commenting, he allows the reader to evaluate the reported events and discussions independently and to judge the appropriateness of Heinrich's reactions. The scene with the crusaders is a case in point: by carefully weighing the words of the knights, the reader will not assume Heinrich's mood but recognize it, as Heinrich himself does later, as an immature reaction. Second, the novel transcends Heinrich's limitations through the sophistication of the author's style. As Novalis observed in connection with Goethe's *Meister*, the hero is a mere "organ" of the poet (III, 639f.); style is in total control of what happens.[7] The language of *Ofterdingen* is not limited to the verbal skill of its protagonist, but in a sense "leads" Heinrich into a preexistent poetic world through the verbal musicality and rhythmic structure of the style. Heinrich slowly internalizes this style and becomes adept at using it, so that his language becomes expressive of a poetic world, which is concretely anticipated also in the inserted narrations and, to a lesser extent, in the poems and the unfinished second part. A fuller understanding of the novel demands that we consider these now, both for their intrinsic value and for what they contribute to the novel's fabric.

III   *Lyrical and Narrative Inserts*

Not counting the dedicatory double sonnet, six of the thirteen songs are contained in the two longer narrative inserts, while the remaining seven are recited by characters in the novel: the knights, Zulima, the miner, the hermit, Schwaning, and Klingsohr. Interestingly, Heinrich, his parents, and Mathilde do not sing. In general, the songs characterize their singer: the knights sing a martial call to liberate the holy grave, Zulima softly and plaintively wonders when her "weary heart" will break under the foreign sky. Schwaning's role song, attributed to young girls, reveals his carefree, light eroticism:

> Allem was die Eltern sprechen,
> Widerspricht das volle Herz.
> Die verbotne Frucht zu brechen
> Fühlen wir der Sehnsucht Schmerz;
> Möchten gern die süßen Knaben
> Fest an unserm Herzen haben. (I, 272)

(Everything the parents say / Is contradicted by our brimming heart./ To break off the forbidden fruit / We feel desire's pain; / Would gladly have the sweet youth / firmly on our bosom.)

The three inserted stories foreshadow the novel's planned transition into a tale (III, 677; and IV, 330); they increase in length and in mythic intensity, but all three demonstrate poetry's orphic transforming power through the active and concrete role songs take in the resolution. The singers and poetic figures prepare Heinrich for his poetic calling, and they anticipate the role Novalis planned for him in the second part of the novel.

The myth of Arion was first told by Herodotus, but Novalis probably adopted it from poems by Tieck and August Wilhelm Schlegel (I, 627): the sailors of a ship want to kill a singer for his jewels, but grant him as a last wish a song. His voice has no effect on them because they plug their ears, but the beasts of the sea are attracted. He jumps into the water and a friendly fish takes him on his back and delivers him to the mainland.

In the next two stories, the orphic songs effect greater changes, indicating poetry's exponential increase in power: in the tale of Atlantis, the poet-protagonist's song softens the heart of a king, while in Klingsohr's tale, the allegorical figure of "Fabel" is instrumental in bringing about a new golden age.

In the second story, poetry mediates between the court of the haughty king of Atlantis and the forest seclusion of a wise man and finally brings together the social classes, decorum and introspection, society and nature. The plot is simple: the king's daughter accidentally meets the wise man's son in the forest; the young people fall in love with each other, and their love is consummated in a cave during a storm. For a year, in which the princess gives birth to a child, the young couple hides with the wise man in the forest, but finally the husband is driven by his love to recite the story of his happiness in the court. The poetic account of the events prepares the reappearance of the king's daughter and grandchild, leading to a final reconciliation.

Neither the plot nor the characters of this story closely resemble those of *Ofterdingen;* however, the inspired birth of the poet through love anticipates Heinrich's story, and the final reconciliation with the king is prophetic of a cosmic transformation that should have taken place in the second part of the novel.

The third narrative insert, Klingsohr's tale, assumes the now familiar triadic historical and cosmological scheme, though it actually describes only the emergence of a final harmony from the middle period. The triple strand of action interlinks three spheres:

the "northern" realm of King Arctur, the middle level of humanity, and the underworld, populated by the Sphinx, the Parcae or sisters of fate, and the tarantulas. The moon is associated with Arctur's "astral" sphere. The fall from the first into the middle period has occurred long before the tale's opening when Sophie (personification of wisdom) had deserted her husband, King Arctur (the "spirit of life"), to descend into the sphere of humanity. In the opening scene, Arctur reigns over a captive frozen kingdom comparable to the frigid sphere of intellect in *Christenheit*, killing time by playing a game of cards with his daughter Freya (peace), which is mysteriously coordinated with the movement and music of star constellations. They ask an attendant old hero to throw his sword into the world as a sign of their readiness for release. The comet-sword crashes against mountains, and one of its splinters drops into a curious group in the human world: Ginnistan (imagination) nurtures her daughter, Fabel, and Fabel's half-brother, Eros, born from the "mother." A scribe incessantly scribbles the father's messages onto sheets of paper, but when Sophie dips these into the water of an altar bowl, they usually emerge empty, indicating that the transcription was senseless. When the father finds the magnetized sword-splinter, the scribe discovers its scientific use as a compass, but Ginnistan bends it into the shape of a curled snake—symbol of sexuality and eternity. Thereupon, the father withdraws to the bedroom "to recuperate from the business of the day" in Ginnistan's arms, and Fabel replaces the scribe, producing scripts that stand the test. Eros, who touched the magnet and momentarily grew up, now prepares for a journey; Sophie permits Ginnistan to accompany him, albeit under the guise of the "mother," not to expose him to temptation.

Their journey leads to Ginnistan's father, the moon, where Eros is led into a treasury to witness a theatrical performance. The opening garden scene first changes into a series of pastoral and romantic landscapes, but the idyls come to an end when the forces of death attack and inflict torture, pain, and death upon all living things. However, chaos and destruction are overcome as inexplicably as they came about:

Suddenly a milk blue stream burst through the dark heap of ashes in every direction. The ghosts wanted to flee but the flood grew visibly and engulfed the hideous brood. Soon all fear was wiped out. Heaven and earth united in the confluence of sweet music. A wonderfully beautiful flower swam glittering on the soft waves. A shimmering arch formed above the stream; divine figures on resplendent thrones sat upon its two sloping sides. Sophie sat highest, the bowl in her hand, next to a magnificent man, with an oak-wreath around her locks and a palm of peace instead of a scepter in her right hand. A lily leaf bent over the cup of the swimming flower; little Fabel sat on it and sang sweet songs to the accompaniment of a harp. Eros himself lay in the cup, bent over a beautiful slumbering girl who kept him tightly embraced. A smaller blossom wound itself around the two, so that they seemed to be transformed into a single flower from the waist down. (I, 300)

With his typically short sentences, Novalis describes in this "play within the play" a clash between the forces of disorder and peace reminiscent of the closing scene of *The Magic Flute*. As in Mozart's opera, evil has no substantiality, and the forces of the underworld disappear instantaneously, as if by a skillful trick of a magician. Klingsohr's tale essentially reenacts the clash of this "magic theater." The show helps Ginnistan to seduce Eros and makes him forget the tasks he set out to accomplish, so that evil becomes rampant at home under the rule of the scribe. Sophie and Fabel escape, the latter by descending into the underworld of the three Parcae, but the mother is eventually burned on the stake and turned into the heap of ashes prefigured in the "magic theater." Her martyrdom helps to overcome evil and to liberate King Arctur's kingdom: in the end, Sophie is reunited with King Arctur, Eros finds the slumbering Freya, the father is mated with Ginnistan, who seems to keep the appearance of the mother, and the mother becomes a hovering guardian spirit. In the final scene, the erotic powers of Ginnistan and Eros are not chastened and subdued, as some interpreters believe, but universalized. Arctur's throne turns into a "luxurious bridal bed," the king embraces his blushing beloved, and the people follow his example by caressing each other. One hears nothing "but tender names and the whisper of kisses" (I, 315)—hardly a festivity of puritans! Fabel's verses close the tale:

> Gegründet ist das Reich der Ewigkeit,
> In Lieb, und Frieden endigt sich der Streit,
> Vorüber ging der lange Traum der Schmerzen,
> Sophie ist ewig Priesterin der Herzen. (I, 315)

(The kingdom of eternity is founded, / In love and peace the strife is bounded, / Gone is the long dream of pain, / Sophie is forever priestess of the hearts.)

Klingsohr's tale admirably conjoins a rich variety of themes and materials from Greek and Nordic mythology, the latest discoveries of science (primarily magnetism and galvanism), and Novalis' Sophie experience. The religious, political, historical, and literary ideas reflect his debt to Jakob Boehme, Goethe, Tieck, Wieland, Schelling, Baader, Ritter, and many others. All these elements, which we shall not be able to trace and elucidate, are incorporated into an unwieldy plot which has a perhaps excessively transparent plan and meaning: the fallen state, dominated by the scribe's "petrified intellect" and lifeless learning, is overcome by Sophie's wise love and Fabel's poetic charm. Unfortunately, this meaning demands that we affix allegorical labels to the characters and become scribe-like interpreters ourselves.

While the message is clear, the forces that move characters and events are not. The splintering of the sword, Eros' journey to the moon, or the events in the "magic theater" seem arbitrary and unmotivated, and the characters often appear as puppets moved by unseen hands. This accords with Novalis' view that poets "worship accidents" (III, 449) and that tales are actually dream images without coherence, ensembles of miraculous things and events (III, 281 and 454). Yet tales are also "the canon of poetry", their representations are "prophetic," "ideal," and "absolutely necessary" (III, 281), as indeed the transformation in Klingsohr's tale is obviously paradigmatic. The formlessness, chaos, and incoherence of a tale are meant to convey that only a confused sense of higher order is available to us. The tale is a higher form of narrative than the realistic novel because, according to Novalis, it no longer "copies nature" (III, 673) but, like poetry, destroys the order of appearances and suggests, but only suggests, another one. "A moral fate, a lawful connection" is against the spirit of the tale (III, 438), yet a higher tale must intimate "some intellect (connection, meaning, etc.)," without "banishing" its spirit (III, 454f.). Thus, the strategy of Klingsohr's tale seems to be to give a mysterious but "prophetic" portrayal of the inevitable transition to a new golden age. Whether Novalis found a balance between order and disorder readers will have to decide for themselves; but we should keep in mind Klingsohr's comment that the tale carries the marks of his youth (I, 287).

IV   *The Conversations*

The discussions in the novel have a philosophical as well as a formal significance in that they explore issues in dialogues which are usually dominated by a teacher-conversant. I single out the topics of dreams, war, history, and poetry for a brief discussion.

Heinrich's awakening from his initial restless dream occasions the novel's first discussion. His father anachronistically takes the enlightened view that "dreams are mere shadows" and that "divine faces" no longer "join our dreams." In advanced ages, direct communication with heaven no longer takes place, God speaks through wise men and saints rather than revelations. But Heinrich insists on the religious and poetic value of dreams: they

seem like a defense against the regularity and triteness of life, like a free recuperation of our constrained imagination, where she jumbles up all of life's images and interrupts the constant seriousness of grown-ups with a joyous play. Without dreams we would surely age faster; and thus we may regard dreams if not as directly given from above at least as a divine provision, a friendly companion during the pilgrimage to the holy grave. (I, 199)

War is the subject of several levels of conversation; first Heinrich is sequentially exposed to the opposing views of the crusaders and the captive Zulima, then he reflects on them in his discussion with Klingsohr. It is a measure of his immaturity that the knights can instill in him enthusiasm for the "wonderful life" of the crusaders, though their scorn of the heathen is reprehensible. The castle's owner boasts with a sword that he took as a spoil from the commander of a surrendered fortress. He killed the owner with his own sword and enslaved his family, whereupon the emperor granted him the privilege of including the sword in his crest. When Heinrich kisses the sword with "fervent devotion" (I, 231), he is told that he too shall be able to enslave beautiful maidens like the one held in the castle. His war euphoria, tainted with sexual violence, quickly evaporates, of course, when the captive Zulima tells her side of the story, but the episode indicates how easily his mind may yet be swayed by his untutored emotions. Later, in his discussion with Klingsohr, he will conclude that war fervor is a "poetic" state incongruous with facts: "War seems to me to have a poetic effect. People believe they have to fight each other for some trivial possessions, not realizing that they are fired by the romantic spirit" (I, 285).

The fifth chapter contains a series of discussions on "Cosmos and Kingdom,"—a title that Elizabeth Sewell has chosen for her sensitive poetic rendering of Heinrich's encounter with the miner and the hermit. As she explains, addressing Novalis:

> I come to you believing there is freedom in both these realms
> Of cosmos and kingdom
>   natural and man-made relations
>   science and history
>   for poet and thinker, who is every man,
>   To move to and fro[8]

These conversations open new spatial, temporal, and psychic dimensions to Heinrich. First he learns that the miners are artists, inasmuch as they get only aesthetic pleasure from what they unearth, and "inverted astrologers" (I, 260), because they construct a past from the earth's prehistoric monuments. Hence, Heinrich's verbal and physical descent into the subterranean world becomes an experience of natural and human history. The cave transports Heinrich into the "fabulous primal ages" (I, 252) when the decaying monstrous animal skeletons were still alive. As if "wandering through the outer courts of earth's inner palace," he realizes with astonishment that another monstrous world could be astir beneath his feet (I, 253). The miner's theory of progressive refinement later interlinks this monstrous past with the human present: nature calmed down, "increasingly intimate harmonies, more peaceful communities, mutual support and animation seem to have formed gradually, and we can look forward to ever better times." The disappearance of monsters and devastating natural catastrophes indicates that nature approaches man, that the exhaustion of her procreative power leads to an increase in her "forming, ennobling, and social powers" (I, 261f.).

When the group encounters in the cave the count Frederick von

Hohenzollern, a hermit, attention shifts from natural to human history. But the count holds the same theory of gradual temporal development, since his contemplative life and his reflections on war and politics represent a refinement over his former physical participation in the destructive crusades:

The true sense for the stories of men develops only late, and more under the quiet influence of memory than under the more powerful impressions of the present. The most immediate events appear loosely connected, but they sympathize all the more miraculously with distant ones; only when one is able to survey a long series and neither take everything literally nor upset the actual order with capricious dreams—only then does one take notice of the secret enchainment of time past and future, and learn to compose history from hope and memory. (I, 257f.)

The hermit's free interchange of "stories" with "history" already indicates that history is a species of poetry for him. He subsequently asserts that "only poets are versed in the art of interlinking events with each other," for "there is more truth in their tales than in learned chronicles. Even if their characters and their fate are invented: the sense in which they are invented is true and natural" (I, 259). Thus, the hermit leads Heinrich from activity (the crusaders) to a reflective and ultimately poetic view of history and prepares him for the discussions with the poet Klingsohr. Indeed, Heinrich's last experience in the hermit's cave is to discover among the books a manuscript which depicts his own past, present, and future (I, 264f.): history turns into a personal fiction; the cosmic journey into the cave leads into the innermost secrets of his life.

Heinrich's conversation with Klingsohr on poetry takes place after the intoxicating evening at Schwaning's house and Heinrich's subsequent dream of losing Mathilde. Overwhelmed by the rich landscape at his feet, Heinrich faces the problem of Goethe's Werther, namely that he is least capable and willing to speak about nature during communion with her (I, 280). Klingsohr's answer is rather different from what one might expect after his drinking song. Emotional and rational approaches to nature are distinct, but poets, who tend to prefer the emotions, should attempt to harmonize them:

cannot urge you strongly enough to support with industry and effort your intelligence, your natural curiosity to know how everything happens and hangs together according to the law of causality. Nothing is more indispensable to a poet than insight into the nature of every affair, acquaintance with the means to attain each goal, and presence of mind to choose the most suitable ones according to time and circumstance. Enthusiasm without intelligence is useless and dangerous, and a poet who is astonished by miracles will do few miracles himself. [. . .] The cool, life-giving warmth of a poetic mind is just the counterpart of the wild heat of a sickly heart. [. . .] A young poet can never be cool and sober enough. Broad, attentive, and quiet disposition belongs to genuine, melodic volubility; speech becomes a confused verbiage if a torrent rages in the breast and dissipates attention into fluttering thoughtlessness. (I, 281)

Remembering his father's sober craftsmanship, Heinrich admits that the self-assurance of technical mastery "produces clearer and more permanent pleasure than unfathomable, exaggerated ecstasy" (I, 282). As if commenting on Novalis' efforts after Sophie's death, Klingsohr remarks that ecstasy should come spontaneously and not as a result of a quest for it; he uses the metaphor of Brownian medicine to assert that ecstasy is beneficial in rare doses, but debilitating and exhausting if experienced frequently.

We cannot tear ourselves fast enough from its residual sweet stupor to return to a routine and exerting activity. It's like with morning dreams, whose somnolent confusion we can escape only by force lest we sink into an increasingly depressing fatigue and drag ourselves through the day in sickly exhaustion. Poetry [. . .] wants to be practiced first and foremost as an exacting art. As mere pleasure it ceases to be poetry. A poet should not run around idly all day, chasing images and feelings. That is completely wrong. A clear and open mind, adroitness in reflection and contemplation, skill in engaging and sustaining all of one's talents in a mutually invigorating activity—these are the requisites of our art. (I, 282)

Klingsohr's message is unambiguous—but is it Novalis' own? Is Klingsohr the model poet, or is he a Goethean figure "who will and must be superseded" (II, 642) by the higher poet of the future? Curiously, Klingsohr's closing words may be taken as a criticism of *Ofterdingen*—a novel for which his own tale provides the blueprint:

If each poet has a unique sphere within which he must stay in order not to lose his breath and composure, there is a definite limit of representability for the totality of human forces as well, beyond which the representation cannot retain its necessary density and shape, and will turn into an empty, deluding chimera. Especially as an apprentice, one can never be sufficiently on guard against such intemperances because lively imaginations all too gladly reach for the limit and seek to grasp and utter presumptuously what is supersensible and extravagant. Only more mature experience will teach us to avoid this incommensurability in subject matters and leave the search of the simplest and highest to philosophic wisdom. [. . .] I would almost say that in all poetry chaos must shimmer through the regular veil of order. [. . .] The best poetry is quite natural to us, and common objects are not seldom its favorite material. For a poet, poetry is restricted to limited means, and just this restriction will turn it into an art. In general, language has a definite sphere. (I, 285f.)

Lest it be thought that this is merely an equivocation on Klingsohr's part, the following two remarks from Novalis' notebooks, written at the time of his preoccupation with *Ofterdingen*, reinforce the view:

One should not represent anything one cannot fully survey, clearly perceive, and completely master—for instance in representing the supernatural. (III, 640)

Sense for poetry has much in common with sense for mysticism. It represents what is unrepresentable, sees the invisible, feels the imperceptible. (III, 685)

It is difficult to escape the conclusion that mystic inspiration on the one hand and insistence on concretion and organization on the other are complementary aspects of the aesthetic theory and practice of Novalis' narrative art. Klingsohr's and Goethe's sobriety are part of Novalis' poetic personality and represent one of the voices in the novel's internal dialogue. In other words, Novalis incorporated into *Ofterdingen* not only a criticism of Goethe but also a Goethean criticism of the most extravagant features of his own novel—a daring and unusual decision consonant with the novel's reflective character. We shall have to turn to the second part to see in what manner he planned to resolve the dialectic.

V *Part II: Fulfillment*

Novalis tackled the second part immediately after finishing the first, but his novel of "time" and "becoming" never reached the stage of "fulfillment." How are we then to imagine its resolution?

About the first part, Novalis remarked to Friedrich Schlegel on
April 5, 1800: "I should be pleased if you find the novel and the
tale happily mixed, and if the first part foretold of an even closer
mixture in the second. The novel should gradually turn into a tale"
(IV, 330). When Schlegel apparently criticized the abrupt transi-
tions, Novalis expressed his "pious hope" for a more supple prose
in the second part and intimated that even its form was to be more
poetic: "Poetry is now born" (IV, 333). Unfortunately, professional
work and the onset of the final sickness in the fall of 1800 allowed
him to write only the opening chapter, entitled "Das Kloster oder
der Vorhof" ("The Monastery, or The Court of Entrance": I, 317–
34), and a few poems and sketches (I, 340–55). Tieck's detailed
account of the remainder (I, 359–69) is based mostly on these fragments, but carries the marks of Tieck's negligent editorship and is
therefore unreliable. Since Novalis' plans were, in any case, not
final, I shall concentrate on the first chapter and not attempt a
detailed reconstruction of the remaining plot.[9]

In keeping with Novalis' plan to open each chapter of the second
part with a poem, the first chapter is prefaced by the verses of a
"sidereal being," Astralis, who was engendered in the sexual pleasure of Heinrich's and Mathilde's first kiss (I, 317). Astralis' birth
coincided with Mathilde's death:

> Ich hob mich nun gen Himmel neugeboren
> Vollendet war das irdische Geschick
> Im seligen Verklärungsaugenblick,
> Es hatte nun die Zeit ihr Recht verloren
> Und forderte, was sie geliehn, zurück. (I, 318)

(Born anew, I rose toward heaven now, / Consummated was earthly fate
/ In the blissful moment of transfiguration; / Time lost then its rights / And
reclaimed what it had loaned.)

An escape from the fetters of temporality is therefore possible, and
the poem's symbolic account of the events once more anticipates
a spaceless and timeless world:

> Eins in allem und alles im Einen
> Gottes Bild auf Kräutern und Steinen
> Gottes Geist in Menschen und Tieren,
> Dies muß man sich zu Gemüte führen.

Keine Ordnung mehr nach Raum und Zeit
Hier Zukunft in der Vergangenheit.
Der Liebe Reich ist aufgetan
Die Fabel fängt zu spinnen an. (I, 318)

(One in all and all in One / God's image on herbs and stones, / God's spirit in men and beasts, / This we must take to heart. / Order is no longer spatial and temporal / Here future is in the past. / Love's empire is open, / Fabel starts to spin.)

As the action resumes, Heinrich is seen roaming the mountains above Augsburg as a pilgrim. His yearning for a sign of divine guidance is satisfied by a visionary experience similar to the one in the third hymn. Mathilde's voice tells him that if he should sing in her honor, a poor girl will approach him and provide him with solace on earth. This poetic reconciliation of Novalis' love for Sophie and Julie leads to Heinrich's spiritual rebirth: he sings the requested praise of Mathilde, and Zyane (*kyanos* = blue cornflower) appears. In the ensuing, sharply punctuated dialogue, she opens Heinrich's eyes to the hidden combinatorial unity underlying his chaotic experience. Suddenly everything is interrelated and full of ambiguity:

Who told you about me?—asked the pilgrim.
Our Mother.
Who is your mother?
The Mother of God.
How long have you been here?
Since my rising from the grave.
Did you die once before?
How could I live otherwise?
Do you live here all alone?
An old man is at home, but I know many more who lived.
Would you like to stay with me?
I like you indeed.
How did you get to know me?
Oh! from the old days; also my former mother used to tell me about you.
Do you have another mother?
Yes, but she is actually the same one.
What was her name?
Maria.

Who was your father?
Count Hohenzollern.
I know him too.
You should know him, since he is your father too.
But I have my father in Eisenach?
You have more parents.
Where are we going then?
Always home. (I, 325)

Accordingly, Zyane leads Heinrich to the sage physician, Sylvester, who looks like the miner, but turns out to be an old acquaintance of Heinrich's father. As he recalls, the father had the talent to become a great artist, but scorned inspiration and turned into an artisan. The remainder of the chapter is a lengthy conversation between Sylvester and Heinrich on earlier themes. The father's uninspired but industrious artisanship apparently proved to be a boon for Heinrich's education, for he was allowed to develop in harmony with his inner potential, whereas most people, according to Sylvester, are "mere leftovers of a full meal despoiled by people of various appetites and taste" (I, 326). Sylvester is a naturalist and primarily interested in the role of nature in education. In the plants, trees, flowers, and clouds, he sees the signs of universal love, but even in thunder and lightning—the miner's monstrous, primordial nature—he recognizes a means of man's education, for the physical threat engenders moral sublimity. Restating the miner's theory, Sylvester claims that evil and suffering will disappear from the world and physical forces turn into moral ones: "There is only one cause of evil—general weakness, and this weakness is nothing but limited moral sensibility and scarcity of stimulation by freedom" (I, 330).

Sylvester claims that conscience cannot be explained, for grasping it would mean having it; in this, as Heinrich remarks, it is like art. Heinrich can therefore understand conscience as the spirit of poetry. Sylvester gives the remarkable reply that

conscience appears in every serious perfection, in every educated truth. Every inclination or skill that reflection transforms into a world view becomes a manifestation, a transmutation of conscience. All education leads to [. . .] freedom. [. . .] This freedom is mastery. The master wields purposeful, free power in a definite and deliberate manner. [. . .] And just this all-embracing freedom, mastery, or sovereignty is the essence, the driving power of conscience. (I, 331).

Heinrich happily accepts this view, since it allows him to attribute
a moral purpose to artistic mastery: "A surprising unity exists between a genuine song and a noble deed" (I, 332).

With this explicit fusion of moral education and poetry, the development toward the envisaged "apotheosis of poetry" (IV, 655)
seems to be set: it leads from novel to tale, from the real world into
a morally superior possible one, from temporality to permanence.
But according to an outline (I, 344), Heinrich was to arrive at this
final stage over a sequence of historical adventures: (1) the face (the
earlier title of the first chapter; the German term *Gesicht* means
both "face" and "vision"), (2) heroic age of chivalry (mostly adventures in Italy), (3) antiquity (visit to Greece), (4) orient (perhaps
travels in North Africa and to Jerusalem), (5) the emperor (probably
at the court of Frederick II in Mainz; there, or at the Wartburg,
the contest of singers would have occurred). Only in the final section, entitled "Die Verklärung" ("Transfiguration"), would the transition from the historical to the mythical world have occurred: here
Heinrich was to free the blue flower from time by destroying the
rule of the sun. The resultant "Marriage of the Seasons" was, according to Tieck, to be celebrated in a major poem of which only
the first introductory lines were written. How would Novalis have
portrayed such an apotheosis of poetry, tale, and myth? Wasn't this
design excessively ambitious? Why didn't Novalis heed Klingsohr's
warning that young poets should not transgress the limits of experience? Some remarks show that he was planning to do just that:
he wanted to move "from the infinite to the finite" (IV, 281) and
to end the novel not like a tale but "with a simple family," in a
"more quiet, simpler, and more humane" manner (I, 345). Indeed,
the further his fictional world moved from reality toward poetry,
myth, and tale, the more concrete its language became. Precisely
the poems and the tales, the most formal and poetic elements of
the novel, contain the most evocative, vivid, and detailed descrip-
tions. The lovers' meeting in the Atlantis story is a case in point:

The sun was beginning to gild the treetops, which swayed with soft mur-
mur, as if they wanted to awaken each other from their nocturnal visions
to jointly greet the sun, when, due to a distant noise, the princess looked
down the path and saw rushing toward her the youth, who noticed her the
very same moment. (I, 219)

Such delicate portrayals and such attention to physical detail are all but absent from the main story, but they are abundant in the other tales, whose unfamiliar settings need concretion. A novel may be abstract, but a tale must be concrete: it must "romanticize" by giving a familiar expression to the unknown and invisible.

We may observe similar features in the poems, especially those intended for the second part. For instance, "Das Lied der Toten" ("Song of the Dead") speaks of the earthly goods in otherworldly festivities:

> Lobt doch unsre stillen Feste,
> Unsre Gärten, unsre Zimmer
> Das bequeme Hausgeräte,
> Unser Hab' und Gut. (I, 351)

(Praise our quiet festivities / Our gardens, our rooms / The comfortable appliances, / Our goods and chattels.)

In the most powerful statement of this new realism, a poem probably intended for the second part, the attack on abstraction is coupled with a vision of a "free life" of songs and kisses:

> Wenn nicht mehr Zahlen und Figuren
> Sind Schlüssel aller Kreaturen
> Wenn die so singen, oder küssen,
> Mehr als die Tiefgelehrten wissen,
> Wenn sich die Welt ins freie Leben
> Und in die freie Welt wird zurückbegeben,
> Wenn dann sich wieder Licht und Schatten
> Zu echter Klarheit wieder gatten,
> Und man in Märchen und Gedichten
> Erkennt die alten wahren Weltgeschichten,
> Dann fliegt von Einem geheimen Wort
> Das ganze verkehrte Wesen fort. (I, 344f.)

(When numbers and figures / Are no longer the key to all creatures, / When those who sing and kiss / Know more than the deeply learned / When the world reverts to free life / And to a free world / If then light and shadow once more / Unite into true clarity, / And in tales and poems one / Recognizes the old true stories of the world / Then one single secret word / Will blow away this whole misbegotten mode of existence.)

VI   *Critical Responses*

The text of the completed sections appeared in the first, 1802, edition of Novalis' works, together with Tieck's report about the plans for the remainder. Schleiermacher thought it was magnificent, Friedrich Schlegel greeted it as a "marvelous and thoroughly new phenomenon" which led poetry back to its sources and reestablished mythology (I, 188f.), and the philosopher Emil Solger agreed that it was "a new and extremely bold attempt to represent poetry through life" and to allow life pass into poetry (I, 190). Count Otto Heinrich von Loeben saw it as a reaffirmation of Catholicism and emulated it in his own *Guido* (1808).

The critical voices were not restricted to the anti-Romantic camp. Achim von Arnim, who read *Ofterdingen* soon after its publication, thought it was a "silly learned peasant prattle" and found it generally "quite mediocre, even miserable," in spite of individual passages of beauty. Klingsohr's tale was boring or insignificant—depending on one's level of understanding.[10] Several years later, he added that poetic works could not originate in the manner of *Ofterdingen's* second part, for they exhausted themselves with the outline.[11] Clemens von Brentano agreed with Arnim's first judgment and replied: "All of its figures have fish tails, all of its flesh is salmon; I sense a strange physical repulsion while reading it."[12]

To be sure, Arnim and Brentano were largely exercising their wit; but even the more serious and sympathetic critics were hesitant. Carlyle did not reckon *Ofterdingen* among Novalis' "most remarkable compositions,"[13] and Maeterlinck thought it was "monochrome" and lacking the "happy audacity" of the fragments—although he praised it as "clear, cold, beautiful, and noble."[14] According to Dilthey, it lacked an energetic shaping force and dissolved everything into a "boundless inwardness," yet he regarded it as the most important early Romantic work, where "a truly magic melody of language" surrounded with unspeakable charm "the profundity of a lonely, noble soul dedicated in earnest to the highest." Even in a later postscript, he challenged Haym's characterization of it as "a dreamily confused image."[15]

Perhaps the greatest admirer of the novel was Hermann Hesse, who described it in an early essay on *Romantik und Neuromantik* (*Romanticism and Neo-Romanticism*, 1900) as a timeless story and dreaming reflection of the soul, "a wing-stroke away from misery and darkness toward the peaks of idea, eternity, salvation." He closed the essay by welcoming every poet who had "something of the soul of Ofterdingen."[16]

Hesse's lyrical and romantic remarks indicate one mode in which Novalis' novel remained effective. I have emphasized its abstract design, verbal structure, and narrative perspective to indicate threads leading in other directions, to Kafka and Thomas Mann. Because of its abstractness and incompleteness, *Ofterdingen* will never attract a large readership, but it will probably continue to elicit admiration from a small band of apprentices and initiates.

CHAPTER 8

End and Beginning

I *The Final Years: 1799–1801*

NOVALIS' second engagement reoriented his life. Upon his return to Weißenfels, shortage of funds became his major problem, and he was therefore eagerly seeking a position to prove himself for rapid advancement. He felt that Freiberg prepared him for technical positions, and he was looking forward to his upcoming tour of the saline works with von Oppel, in the hope that this influential man would become his sponsor in Dresden (IV, 283). The tour, which took place in late May and early June 1799, was indeed successful, and upon the strong recommendation of von Oppel, Novalis was appointed in December as assessor and fourth member of the Weißenfels Salt Directorate, which was chaired by his father. The annual salary was a meager four hundred talers, one hundred less than he expected (IV, 284).

The summer and autumn of 1799 proved to be eventful. New notebooks were started, *Christenheit*, a few *Lieder*, and other poems were completed. Among the latter was a witty poem depicting his mother on her fiftieth birthday as a grapevine at vintage. Frequent trips led to new acquaintances: in July Novalis met Ludwig Tieck in Jena, and the sudden, intense friendship provided him with new poetic inspiration. During a visit to Freiberg in August, he met Henrik Steffens, the Norwegian *Naturphilosoph*. Steffens was unhappy with Novalis' approach to nature at the time, but forty years later he remembered a transfigured Novalis, a poet, whose eyes radiated "ethereal blaze" and whose life dissolved "in a deep myth" (IV, 639f.). At the Jena meeting of the Romantics in November, Novalis finally met Johann Wilhelm Ritter, the young physicist whose work on galvanism had led him to exclaim in an earlier letter:

"Ritter [=knight] is a knight and we are mere pages" (IV, 275). The first encounter, movingly recalled in Ritter's reminiscences (IV, 650–52), turned into a lasting friendship. Novalis secured some financial help for Ritter (IV, 319ff.) and became fascinated by the promises of research on galvanism. Galvani had discovered that frog legs twitched when they were used to close an electric circuit, and he believed, with many others, that this was due to a galvanic life force inherent in the organism. Volta's view that the twitching resulted from an electric current generated by the potential difference between the different metals in the circuit gained only slow acceptance. Novalis, who depicted galvanic actions in Klingsohr's tale, hoped that galvanism would turn out to be a fundamental force of nature. In his view, Ritter's endless experiments and bold speculation were in search of "the actual world soul of nature" (III, 655).

From the end of November until shortly before Christmas, Novalis stayed in Artern, doing official business and working on *Ofterdingen*. His creative spurt continued during the first months of 1800: the *Hymnen* were completed in January, the first part of the novel on April 5. Philosophy was now "idling on his bookshelves"; with the help of Boehmean mysticisms a "powerful spring with its welling, driving, constructing, and mixing forces" (IV, 322), he happily left "these icebergs of pure reason" behind (IV, 321). The Boehmean debt was gratefully acknowledged in a poem dedicated "To Tieck," which tells of an encounter between a boy and Boehme, author of the book the boy finds on a "decaying bench" in a "desolate garden." The boy inherits Boehme's *Aurora* and Boehme's hope for a new dawn:

> Verkündiger der Morgenröte,
> Des Friedens Bote sollst du sein.
> Sanft wie die Luft in Harf' und Flöte
> Hauch' ich dir meinen Atem ein. (I, 412)

(Proclaimer of dawn, / Emissary of peace shall you become. / Gently, like the breeze in harps and flutes, / I infuse you with my breath.)

The Boehmean spring engendered a plan to write an essay on the mystic (III, 646) and left its mark on several poems written in the spring of 1800.

The few surviving papers relating to Novalis' professional work give a clear testimony to his competence and dedication. There exists, for instance, a remarkable, longer memorandum in which he thoughtfully attempts to reconcile the differences between his father and Friedrich Senf, another member of the directorate. Senf felt frustrated by the conservatism of Novalis' father and asked for greater independence. Novalis opposed Senf's request because he feared it would endanger the directorate's collective decisionmaking, but he thought that Senf's reform zeal was a healthy counterbalance for his father's "steady opposition to new propositions; his hesitancy and prudence in communications, decisions, and reports; his anxious attention to accuracy in budget and estimates; and his ascetic strictness and mistrust of subordinates" (III, 758f.). The statement was diplomatically skillful and not uncritical of the father, who was, after all, Novalis' superior.

The duties of Novalis' position involved a number of special assignments, the first of which was to survey and describe the lignite deposits and their mining within the directorate's jurisdiction, with an eye to the eventual replacement of wood by lignite in heating and purifying salt. Novalis gave a lengthy and careful report on the situation in a private letter to Werner on April 28, 1800 (III, 773–90). He listed all the mines, vividly and exactly described their mode of production, characterized the ownership and the quality of the lignite, and finally gave a detailed portrayal of how the briquettes of lignite were produced.

Novalis' most important achievement was to participate in Werner's comprehensive geological survey of Saxony, which aimed at theoretical insights and, even more so, at the discovery and mapping of mineral and energy resources. Werner established nine teams, each consisting of two of his advanced students. Although Novalis did not complete a full course of study at Freiberg, he was appointed head of the team charged with the survey of an area south of Leipzig. He completed the assignment (on foot!) with his assistant, F.M.T. Haupt, within two weeks and sent a preliminary report to Werner on June 10 (III, 794–98). Because of his subsequent illness, the final report, which Werner singled out for praise in his comprehensive account, was submitted by Haupt only in 1802. The project represented a milestone in Saxony's geological survey and served as a model for similar efforts elsewhere.

When Novalis undertook the survey, he had already applied for the post of *Amtshauptmann* for Weißenfels, Heldrungen, and Sachsenburg. The *Amtshauptmann* was an honorary circuit director, and

Novalis had to state expressly that he could continue as assessor, since the territories overlapped. But he took the job seriously, and in applying, he already singled out the construction of a highway to Frankfurt/Oder as the project to which he intended to give special attention. On September 28 he submitted the required sample decision, which virtually assured him of the job, and soon left for Dresden. Upon receiving the news that his brother Bernhard had drowned on October 29, he had a violent hemoptysis, which radically worsened his already unstable health. His appointment to the supernumerary position of circuit directorship finally came through on December 6, but he was already in the last stages of his illness and could no longer effectively assume the post. On January 20 he was transported back to Weißenfels by his father and Julie; on March 25 he died in the presence of Friedrich Schlegel and his brother Karl. His death was not only a loss to German literary life, it also deprived Saxony of one of its promising civil servants.

Novalis' steady dedication to his professional duties should dispel the legend that he was unfit for life, but it does raise a question about the relationship between the carefully observing, describing, and calculating government official and the poet who satirized a vicious scribe and his senseless notes in Klingsohr's tale. Opinions differ on this matter.[1] Unlike Kafka, Mallarmé, and other modern writers, Novalis did not consider his civil career a danger to his poetic calling; he wrote many "occasional" poems which celebrated the events of everyday life, the birthdays, the purchase of a garden (I, 396), or just a merry evening with punch (I, 391). He thought that even office work can be treated poetically and wished for "deep poetic meditation to carry out the transformation" (III, 654) of everyday life into poetry. He attempted to achieve this by giving poetic accounts of his spiritual development and by deliberately molding life itself through the power of imagination. In the "occasionality" of his poetry and the "poetry" of his life lies the reciprocal unity between his life and art. Still there remains a discrepancy between his civic and visionary selves, even if he himself did not admit it. The man who expected a revolutionary transformation of the world through the imagination in *Christenheit* could also speak with the voice of an engineer: "I am convinced that true revelations are more easily accessible to a cold, technical intellect and calm moral sense than to fantasy, which seems to lead us merely into the realm of ghosts, this antipode of true heaven" (III, 578).

II *Last Thoughts on Final Questions*

Novalis' last striking meditations encircle sensuality, love, disease, and sin in a complex fashion. Some glorify the human body, justifying Thomas Mann's later tour de force of associating him with Walt Whitman:

One should seek God among men. In human affairs, in human thoughts and sensations does the spirit of heaven reveal itself most clearly.[. . .] There is but one temple in the world—the human body. Nothing is more sacred than this noble shape. Bowing to men is homage to this revelation in the flesh. (Divine worship of the lingam, of the breast of statues.) We touch heaven when we run our fingers over a human body. (III, 565f.)

Here, as in the hymn of the *Lieder*, pantheism is reaffirmed; the organ of desire is also the source of universal love and of religion (see also III, 488, 523, and 570).

But elsewhere Novalis explored the problematic aspects of eroticism. Not that he was under the sway of the sixth commandment; he was against "hiding external nature behind artificial covers," being ashamed of "candid nature," or keeping sexual urges suppressed (III, 560). In a personal, and historically surely incorrect, way he regarded Christianity as the "religion of sensuality" (III, 653) which abolished sin and "all belief in contrition and atonement" (III, 563). But he was keenly aware of the destructiveness of sexuality: sexual pleasure was the basis of cruelty (III, 655); sexual desire, the yearning for physical touch, and the pleasure at the sight of naked bodies indicated an "appetite for human flesh" (III, 575); sensuality, religion, and cruelty had an intimate relationship and a common tendency (III, 568).

Novalis retained to the end of his life the view that sin and evil were merely the by-products of freedom. In the last notes, however, this view acquires a novel interpretation: "There has been one disease only and thereby only one universal medicine. With sensibility, and its organs, the nerves, disease entered nature. Thus freedom and willfulness were brought into nature, and thereby offense against the will of nature, the cause of all evil" (III, 657). Disease is "bodily madness" (III, 586), then, sinful deviation from the norm. By extension, evolution is not a positive striving, but a series of transgressions where each higher state is a sick mutation of the preceding lower state:

All diseases resemble sin inasmuch as they are transcendences. All our diseases are phenomena of a heightened sensibility which wants to change into higher forces. When man wanted to become God, he sinned. Diseases of plants are animalizations. Diseases of animals are rationalizations. Diseases of stones—vegetations. (III, 662f.)

Disease belongs to individualization. (III, 681).

These striking ideas represent a counterpart to the theories of Sylvester and the miner in *Ofterdingen* and seem to anticipate the meditations of Nietzsche and others on heightened sensibility, disease, decadence, and artistic genius. Novalis' position is ambiguous. On the one hand, he felt that man should follow nature's ways and that his sensibility, his spiritual deviation from physical nature, and his desire to become God are sinful. Yet on the other, the urge to grow, to change into higher forms of life may itself be "unnatural," and the moral control of fallen nature is necessary: "Our elements drive toward desoxidation. Life is a forced oxidation" (III, 687). Hence, natural and moral striving are distinct.

In the last *Hymnen,* in the *Lieder,* in his late poetry and notes, Novalis seems to be striving for a religious and stoic state of mind which suppresses all natural striving:

Stationary nature is inexplicable; it can only be explained in motion toward morality. (III, 601)

The system of morality must become the system of nature. (III, 662)

Spiritually disposed man is inactive to the point of passion. (III, 489)

All activity ceases when knowledge takes over. The state of knowing is happiness, blessed peace of contemplation—heavenly quietism. (III, 594)

Diseases distinguish man from animals and plants—man is born to suffer. The more helpless, the more receptive to morality and religion. (III, 667)

Morality, properly understood, is man's actual medium of life. It is essentially identical with fear of God. Our pure ethical will is the will of God. (III, 684)

Diary entries made between April 15 and October 16, 1800, indicate that in this sense, Novalis saw his own illness as "years of apprenticeship towards a higher art of life" and as "studies in the control of disposition" (IV, 58). Overcoming anxiety and physical suffering, cheerful acceptance of the inevitable were his goals:

When we steadily think of the endless uncertainty of human wealth, we must ultimately become indifferent and courageous. All anxiety comes from the devil; courage and cheerfulness are from God. [. . .] Ill fate is a calling to [serve] God. Only through bad fortune can one become holy, which is why the ancient saints threw themselves into calamity. (IV, 54f.)

With moving simplicity and persistence, these diaries ask not for freedom from pain but for serenity facing it:

If the soul is at peace, the body will soon be pacified as well (IV, 55).

Today I had an extremely blessed day. Only in the morning a few gentle fits of anxiety. Subsequently all day long inexpressibly calm, strong, courageous, free, and relaxed (IV, 56).

As soon as I strengthened my stomach I became inexpressibly calm and serene. [. . .] Peace is the true condition of man. For the peaceful man every external situation is tolerable and even pleasant. [. . .] I may expectorate blood for a long time—but what do I gain by becoming anxious each time anew? Anxiety damages, courage strengthens.[. . .] The will of God be done—not mine (IV, 57).

The poetic lines written to Just in November 1800 sum up Novalis' final striving for peace: "When physical discomfort does not disorient me, which does not happen that frequently, my disposition is clear and quiet. Religion is the great Orient in us, which is seldom stirred up. Without it I would be unhappy. This way, everything unites in one great peaceful thought, in one quiet, eternal faith" (IV, 341f.).

III *Image and Legacy*

The history of Novalis' legacy is a chronicle of changing reactions to German Romanticism. After his death, the first Romantic group disbanded. The later Romantics in Dresden, Berlin, Heidelberg, or Munich followed distinctly different paths. The Napoleonic wars killed the remainder of revolutionary fervor, weakened cosmopolitanism, and fostered the rise of that German nationalism which, in turn, led to a renewed interest in the national heritage and folklore. Here lay the foundations of Arnim and Brentano's *Des Knaben Wunderhorn* (1806–1808), a collection of folksongs, and the fairytales of the Grimm brothers. The sympathy for Catholicism led many, including Friedrich Schlegel and two of Novalis' brothers, to a formal conversion; the corresponding conservatism in politics was typified by Adam Müller's theory of state.[2] The unique symbiosis of poetry and philosophic reflection in early Romanticism all but disappeared. Of the later Romantic writers, only Joseph von Eichendorff may be compared to Novalis in poetic and religious intensity. E.T.A. Hoffmann, though he created myths and saturated his stories with science or pseudoscience, had neither Novalis' philosophical acuity nor his faith, and he often merely exploited Romantic themes and concerns to create suspenseful stories which were full of ironies and ambiguities.

The changing nature of Romanticism determined Novalis' image, since Tieck and Friedrich Schlegel decided what should be included in the editions of his works. By willfully truncating and arranging his notes, they obscured the logic of Novalis' thought and established the image of an oracular prophet and an aphoristic wit so that Brentano could remark that his fragments looked like a universe butchered and stretched on the floor, with entrails numbered and placed under an index.[3] Tieck's biographical preface to the 1814 edition used material from a biography by Novalis' brother Karl and added mostly cheap color which helped perpetuate the Novalis legend. Just's considerably more sober biography (1805) could not redress the balance. Justinus Kerner, for instance, was shocked by the realization that Novalis was actually a conscientious bureaucrat, and only the reconfirmation that his "death was beautiful" could console him (IV, 550). Already in 1805, Joseph Görres celebrated Novalis as a "true mystic" and as the "herald of the legacy for a better world"; a year later, Zacharias Werner remarked that only Novalis was a true saint among the new ones, while Adam Müller asserted that the "divinatory spirit of the incomparable Novalis" was among the greatest in the eighteenth century.[4] By 1817, the Brockhaus Encyclopedia spoke of a "divine youth" with "heavenly appearance," "who wandered on earth only to soar soon again up to the beloved country of his yearning."[5]

Such adulation inevitably elicited hostile reactions. Goethe correctly sensed that many celebrants of Novalis' Romantic genius indirectly attacked his own Classical taste and questioned his authority. Already irritated by Novalis' published criticism of *Wilhelm Meister,* he mistakenly assumed that Novalis had also converted to Catholicism and included him in a famous attack he reportedly made on the Romantics on April 17, 1808. Noting that some recent articles had raised Friedrich Schlegel to the role of a new "imperator" of literature, he added:

Novalis was no [imperator] yet, but with time he too could have become one. A pity he died so young, especially since he pleased his age and became catholic. According to newspapers, flocks of girls and students made pilgrimages to his grave and strewed flowers for him with full hands. I'd call that a good beginning, and one may expect good things to follow. Since I am not much of a newspaper reader, I ask my friends present to inform me immediately should something further of that sort, something of importance, a canonization or the like, happen.[6]

Only ignorance of the context could have led many commentators to believe that Goethe intended to praise Novalis. He called him a potential imperator because he saw a link between Novalis' *Wilhelm Meister* critique and the literary diatribes of his own day, and even after lengthy conversations with Just in 1816, he was unable to form a more favorable view of him.

Goethe's hostility and irony was shared by others. Franz Grillparzer, who equated Novalis with a "worship of dilettantism," thought it was the ill fate of Germany to place such a high value on "this swaying dreaming, this image and conceptless prescience," and concluded: "let monks and hermits chime with the Hymns to the Night, light is for active men."[7] He surely did not know that by asking that this "numb, dreamy state of mind" be overcome, he was almost verbatim quoting Kingsohr's admonition to Heinrich.

The younger generation, especially the politically and socially conscious members of the Young Germany movement, tended to agree with Grillparzer. Heinrich Laube, for instance, regarded Novalis as a "genuine bird of paradise of whom it is said that he is without feet and must always float in the air.[. . .] The seed of an early death [. . .] attuned his organs to seraphical flights, purified every impulse to disembodied ecstasy."[8] Laube's words echo Heinrich Heine's *Romantische Schule (Romantic School,* 1835), where Novalis was ranked below Hoffmann because of his constant "hovering in blue air." In a half mocking, half sympathetic tone, Heine considered Novalis' poetry as disease and his life "merely a dreamy pining away."[9]

During the first half of the nineteenth century, the most insightful assessment of Novalis appeared in Eichendorffelel's history of modern German literature. Eichendorff wrote from a decidedly Catholic point of view without being dogmatic. He was the first to point out that Novalis did not turn away from reality even though he envisaged a hegemony of poetry. Especially in *Ofterdingen*, he attempted to grasp "real life" with its worldly relations, of marriage, state, and trade.[10] According to Eichendorff, Novalis was the first to state in public "that all modern education was rooted in Christianity and had to lead back to its foundations."[11] His strategy was to reawaken the religious spirit from its prosaic slumber through the power of poetry, for he understood poetry "in its most magnificent, general meaning" as being almost identical with religion.[12] But Eichendorff's admiration was tempered by just reservations. First, poetic religion could easily reduce religion to poetry, as actually happened with many of Novalis' followers; second, Novalis ultimately wavered in his affirmation of Catholicism: prophecy mingled with doubt, faith in the church with barely concealed pantheism. He envisaged above Christianity a higher church which was to encompass all the religions of all times; but as his cathedral rose into the air, his faith started to talk in two tongues.[13]

Eichendorff's essay offered a new perspective on Novalis' religion and religious poetry, but it was perhaps the last look Romanticism took at itself. The next serious student of Novalis was the philosopher Wilhelm Dilthey, in 1865. Dilthey's excessive reliance on Tieck led him to conclude that Novalis was a pawn in the hand of fate to whom the pinnacle of greatness in objectivity was denied. But he wished to change the common image by attempting to show that Novalis' fragments were "perhaps not quite so random and without connection, his Ofterdingen not so boundlessly vague" as they appeared to his former critics.[14] To make his case, Dilthey jettisoned Novalis' claims as a scientist and considered his scientific ideas as mere stepping stones toward a poetic approach to nature.[15] Thus, Novalis' ideas became important for Dilthey for their metaphysics and their contribution to a theory of the humanities which Dilthey himself tried to construct.[16] This approach not only prepared the way toward late revaluations of Novalis, it also revealed the threads leading from Novalis to Schopenhauer, Wagner, and Nietzsche—a matter which unfortunately cannot be pursued here.

Thomas Carlyle's great review essay of the 1826 edition was superior to all German criticism written prior to Eichendorffelel's, even though it portrays Novalis as a strange, lunar spirit. Carlyle obviously admired and respected this "most ideal of all Idealists,"[17] but he confessed to have "but a feeble notion" of his "truly wonderful subtlety of intellect"[18] which he found abstruse and extremely difficult to penetrate.[19] Keeping his English audience in mind, Carlyle urged sensibly but perhaps too defensively that readers should not give up too early on Novalis, for even Coleridge's *Friend* and his *Biographia Literaria* were "but a slight business" compared to Novalis' "unfathomed mine of philosophical ideas."[20] He preferred the fragments, for although he found "pure religious temper, and heartfelt love of Nature" in the poetry,[21] this revealed to him "no great skill or practice," merely "indubitable prolixity," "languor," and a "low-voiced, not unmelodious monotony."[22] In spite of passivity, "undue softness," and "want of rapid energy,"[23] Novalis could be seen as a German Pascal. Maeterlinck later amended the analogy to read: "a Pascal, slightly somnambulistic."[24]

Carlyle's pioneering essay was instrumental in getting English poets and American Transcendentalists interested in Novalis.[25] Emerson owned a copy of the 1842 *Ofterdingen* translation and borrowed from the library his collected works, but he relied primarily on Carlyle's translations and remarks, and he thought that Carlyle himself exemplified Novalis' idea of the union between poetry and philosophy.[26] In his lecture on Goethe (1844), he gave a remarkably judicious sketch of how "the ardent and holy Novalis" reacted to Goethe's *Meister*.[27] Margaret Fuller was among the few Americans who read Novalis in the original. She had a deep affinity with him and admired especially his faith and his poetic approach to nature. Apparently she copied one of Novalis' hymns onto the flyleaf of her Bible.[28] Unfortunately little is known about Edgar Allan Poe's familiarity with Novalis,[29] though he came to be admired by the French Symbolists for many ideas that Novalis had explored first.

Indeed, the French Symbolists inherited their forms, themes, and issues from early German rather than French Romanticism.[30] Abandonment of mimesis in favor of evocation and preoccupation with inwardness, emancipation of poetic from everyday language, imaginative reconstruction of the world through chance and calculation in a musical and algebraic language, thematic preoccupation with night and death, disease and decadence, eroticism and inwardness—these were but a few characteristics of the new French poetry which were anticipated by Novalis with major force. One has to remember, however that Baudelaire, Rimbaud, Mallarmé, or Valéry no longer had allegiance to Christianity and German Idealism.[3]

In the last decade of the nineteenth century, Novalis suddenly became widely read in France. André Gide read *Die Lehrlinge* in Munich (1892) and adopted the description of the child novice in a passage of his novel *Le voyage d'Uriel (The Voyage of Uriel,* 1893).[32] He planned to translate *Ofterdingen*, but this task was carried out by others. In 1893, Henri Albert published a translation of Klingsohr's tale. In 1895, Maurice Maeterlinck published his translation of *Die Lehrlinge* together with some fragments and a lengthy introductory study. Next to Carlyle's, it is to date the most important document on Novalis' impact upon foreign writers.

For Maeterlinck, Novalis demonstrated that "we possess a Self more profound and more inexhaustible than the Self of passions or of pure reason."[33] Recognizing Novalis' scientific and philosophical bent, he thought of him as a "scientific mystic" who never entered "the narrow prisons of systematic philosophy" and dealt with science only "at moments, and at places where it was on the point of being confounded with poetry."[34] Maeterlinck further "poeticized" Novalis' life and death, but he was successful in stimulating interest in his poetic works; the Symbolists, among them Paul Gérardy, Erwin Rodenbach, Edmond Barthélemy (the translator of Carlyle's Novalis essay), came to regard Novalis as a kindred soul. Through the French Symbolists, Novalis eventually regained respect among the German poets, especially in the circle around Stefan George. The final phase of that Symbolist and neo-Romantic Novalis revival was perhaps marked by a poem dedicated to Novalis by the Austrian poet Georg Trakl:

> In dunkler Erde ruht der heilige Fremdling.
> Es nahm von sanftem Munde ihm die Klage der Gott,
> Da er in seiner Blüte hinsank.

Eine blaue Blume
Fortlebt sein Lied im nächtlichen Haus der Schmerzen.[35]

(In dark earth rests the holy stranger / The lament was taken from his gentle mouth by the God, / As he succumbed in his prime. / A blue flower / Survives his song in the nightly house of suffering.)

Of the twentieth-century reactions to Novalis, which concern mostly his novels and theoretical writings, Hermann Hesse's and Thomas Mann's may be singled out as representative. Hesse's early admiration for Novalis and his *Ofterdingen* deepened in the course of his life. In a Postcript to a volume of documents on his life, Hesse characterized Novalis as one of the noblest modern geniuses in Germany and author of the "most wondrous and arcane work known in German cultural history."[36] Inevitably, Novalis loomed large in Hesse's own works, primarily in *Der Steppenwolf* and *Das Glasperlenspiel (The Glass Bead Game)*.[37] Hesse, who portrayed himself as Klingso(h)r, adopted Novalis' "magical conception of life" and his "path to inwardness" and used these as themes and artistic means in his novels. In quest of their true selves, his heroes are in a constant process of negotiating between the demands of the world and their own spiritual aspirations.

Thomas Mann had a more complex and critical attitude. Although he was deeply indebted to the Romantic tradition of Schopenhauer, Wagner, and Nietzsche, he turned to Novalis only once he became critical of this tradition for political reasons. In a 1922 speech he came to the defense of the Weimar Republic by calling upon the authority of Novalis to make the republic palatable to the conservative German audience and by associating this "sensuous thinker and highly intellectual dreamer"[38] with Walt Whitman. The two made admittedly a "strange couple," but the daring association was not without justification: Mann recognized that Novalis' formal espousal of the monarchy contained republican elements, that the "knight of the blue flower" was also a utopian, a progressivist, and a man of the Enlightenment. He correctly saw a link to Whitman in Novalis' "political pantheism" and "social eroticism," although he was less convincing in suggesting that Novalis' religious faith could readily be replaced by Mann's own brand of secular humanism. Mann's deeper affinity with Novalis was revealed in a parenthetical remark of the speech to the effect that one could write a *Bildungsroman*, where the encounter with death becomes the experience of life—a reference to his *Zauberberg (Magic Mountain)*, then in progress, which came to be saturated with themes and ideas from Novalis. Suffice it to mention the encyclopedic form, the conversational structure, the thematic use of science, or the association between disease, love, and death.

Mann's later speech *Über Deutschland und die Deutschen (On Germany and the Germans*, 1945) indicates that the rise of Nazi power further alienated him from the Romantic tradition, which he now saw as a major culprit in the problems of modern Germany. Yet his last novels show how deep his ties to this tradition were. With *Doktor Faustus*, he wrote an agonizing Nietzschean book on art, disease, and politics; his last and unfinished novel, *Felix Krull*, is a comic variation on the Romantic themes of art and life, of man's organic unity and sympathy with the cosmos. In writing on these themes he may not have relied directly on Novalis. But Novalis is among the great creative and disseminating minds of modernity whose ideas have become deeply embedded in the intellectual and artistic heritage of our age. To convey a sense of this vitality has been my purpose.

Notes and References

Preface

1. Richard Faber, *Novalis: Die Phantasie an die Macht* (Stuttgart: Metzler, 1970), p. 11.
2. Peter Berglar, "Geschichte und Staat bei Novalis," *Jahrbuch des freien deutschen Hochstifts*, 1974, p. 154.
3. Georg Lukács, for instance, wrote an early appreciative essay on Novalis ("Zur romantischen Lebensphilosophie: Novalis" in Lukács, *Die Seele und die Formen* [Berlin: Fleischel, 1911], 93–117), but rejected him after his espousal of Marxism. Hans Mayer condemns Novalis almost for the same reasons for which Berglar praises him (*Von Lessing bis Thomas Mann. Wandlungen der bürgerlichen Literatur in Deutschland* [Pfullingen: Neske, 1959], p. 25). Until recently, the general silence of GDR critics and historians on Novalis has been interrupted only by occasional attacks on him and on "bourgeois" interest in him.

Chapter One

1. Novalis, *Schriften*, ed. Paul Kluckhohn and Richard Samuel, 2nd. ed. (Stuttgart: Kohlhammer, 1960–1975), IV, 531. Further documentation for texts in this edition (including texts by other authors reprinted in it) will be in the body of my book. For vol. I I am using the 3rd ed. of 1977.
2. Friedrich Schleiermacher remarked: "I do not believe that he chose his beloved correctly, or, rather, that he had found her; I am almost convinced, she would not have sufficed him, had she stayed alive" (I, 188).
3. Cf. Thomas Carlyle: "We cannot but think that some result precisely similar in moral effect might have been attained by many different means; nay, that by one means or another, it would not have failed to be attained" ("Novalis," *Critical and Miscellaneous Essays* [New York: Scribners, 1899], II, 15).
4. Hans Wolfgang Kuhn observes that Novalis mentions only moments of enthusiasm and happiness, but not an actual vision: *Der Apokalyptiker und die Politik* (Freiburg: Rombach, 1961), p. 67.

Chapter Two

1. The two works on the *Wissenschaftslehre* were *About the Concept of the Science of Knowledge* (*Über den Begriff der Wissenschaftslehre*,

1794) and *Grounds of the Science of Knowledge* (*Grundlage der gesamten Wissenschaftslehre*, 1794–1795).

2. Johann Gottlieb Fichte, *Ausgewählte Werke*, ed. Fritz Medicus (Darmstadt: Wissenschaftliche Buchgesellschaft, 1962), III, 16.

3. Ibid., III, 18.

4. Ibid., I, 227.

5. Ibid., I, 329.

6. Ibid., I, 292.

7. Ibid., I, 437.

8. Ibid., I, 298 and 305 respectively.

9. Ibid., I, 453.

10. Hermann August Korff, *Geist der Goethezeit*, 6th ed. (Leipzig: Koehler, 1964), III, 246.

11. Samuel Taylor Coleridge, *Biographia Literaria*, Everyman's Library (London: Dent, 1965), p. 167.

12. *Kritische Friedrich Schlegel Ausgabe*, ed. Ernst Behler (Paderborn: Schöningh, 1958–), II, 173.

13. Novalis, II, 387. Kant's statement appears in the Preface to the second edition of the *Kritik der reinen Vernunft* (Riga: Hartknoch, 1787), p. xxx.

14. Schlegel, xii, 338.

15. These manuscripts relate to Fichte's *Grundriß des Eigentümlichen der Wissenschaftslehre* (1795) and *Grundlage der gesamten Wissenschaftslehre* (1794–1795).

16. Kant, *Metaphysische Anfangsgründe der Naturwissenschaft* (Riga: Hartknoch, 1786), p. x.

17. Wilhelm Dilthey, "Novalis" (1865), in Dilthey, *Das Erlebnis und die Dichtung* (rpt. Göttingen: Vandenhoeck & Ruprecht, 1965), p. 213.

18. Kant, *Kritik der reinen Vernunft*, p. xxf.

19. Ibid., p. xiii.

20. See Heinz Moenkemeyer, *François Hemsterhuis* (New York: Twayne, 1975).

21. François Hemsterhuis, *Lettre sur l'homme*, ed. Georges May (New Haven: Yale University Press, 1964), p. 458.

22. Schlegel, II, 85.

23. Friedrich Wilhelm Joseph Schelling, *Ideen zu einer Philosophie der Natur* (1797), in *Sämmtliche Werke*, ed. K.F.A. Schelling (Stuttgart: Cotta, 1856–61), II, 56.

24. *Von der Weltseele*, in Schelling, II, 564.

25. Gustav Plitt, *Aus Schellings Leben* (Leipzig: Hirzel, 1869–70), I, 431.

26. This accords with Henrik Steffens' report to Schelling about his first meeting with Novalis. Steffens complained that Novalis had no scientific discipline, and tended to make Schlegelian witty remarks about nature. He

was also guilty of postulating a primal infinitude instead of a polarity in nature (IV, 637).

27. Kant, *Kritik der reinen Vernunft*, xxf., and Schelling, I, 166.

28. Schlegel, II, 197.

29. Rainer Maria Rilke, *Duino Elegies*, translated, introduced, and commented, J. B. Leishman and Stephen Spender (New York: Norton, 1939), p. 61.

Chapter Three

1. Coleridge, p. 167.

2. Percy Bysshe Shelley, "A Defense of Poetry," *Selected Poetry and Prose*, ed. Carlos Baker (New York: Random House, 1951), p. 517.

3. Johann Wolfgang Goethe, "Maximen und Reflexionen" no. 752, *Werke* (Hamburg: Wegner, 1948–60), XII, 471.

4. William Blake, "Auguries of Innocence," *The Portable Blake*, ed. Alfred Kazin (New York: Viking, 1946), p. 150.

5. Kant, *Metaphysische Anfangsgründe*, p. viii.

6. Kant's argument was recapitulated in Friedrich Murhard's mathematical textbook from which Novalis prepared excerpts and notes (III, 119–24).

7. Cf. *Gottfried Wilhelm Leibniz, Mathematische Schriften*, ed. C. I. Gerhardt IV (1859; rpt. Hildesheim: Olms, 1962), 459ff.

8. Schlegel, II, 182f. On Schlegel's concept of "Universalpoesie" see Hans Eichner's *Friedrich Schlegel* (New York: Twayne, 1970).

9. The first sentence of this passage became the epigraph in one of the most important modern treatises on the scientific method, Karl Popper's *The Logic of Scientific Discovery* (first edition in German: *Logik der Forschung* [Vienna: Springer, 1935]).

10. Korff, III, 247.

11. Coleridge, p. 168f.

Chapter Four

1. Ralph Freedman (*The Lyrical Novel* [Princeton: Princeton University Press, 1963]) sees Novalis as pioneer of this genre. According to Freedman, in the lyrical novel "the usual scenery of fiction becomes a texture of imagery, and characters appear as *personae* for the self" (p. 1); it "absorbs action altogether and refashions it as a pattern of imagery" (p. 2); the world "is conceived, not as a universe in which men display their actions, but as a poet's vision fashioned as a design. The world is reduced to a *lyrical point of view*, the equivalent of the poet's 'I' " (p. 8). These statements are highly applicable to *Die Lehrlinge* and *Ofterdingen*.

2. Wilhelm Dilthey was the first to claim that Novalis planned a positive

resolution for the competing views of nature (Dilthey, p. 230f. and 324). Several recent critics have identified strict compositional and structural principles underlying the text. According to Jurij Striedter, the first chapter has a tripartite arrangement, where the voices become increasingly more personal ["Die Komposition der 'Lehrlinge zu Sais,'" *Der Deutschunterricht*, 7 (1955), 5–23]; according to Ulrich Gaier, a sevenfold *Konstruktionsprinzip* underlies the *Novices* and indeed many of Novalis' other works (*Krumme Regel. Novalis' 'Konstruktionslehre des schaffenden Geistes' und ihre Tradition* (Tübingen: Niemeyer, 1970], esp. pp. 7–108); Géza von Molnár found the organizational principle in the Kantian categories of understanding ("The Composition of Novalis' 'Die Lehrlinge zu Sais': A Reevaluation," *PMLA*, 85 [1970], 1002–14).

3. Schiller's essay on *The Mission of Moses* (*Die Sendung Moses*, 1790) attributes Moses' founding of monotheism to his training as an Egyptian priest and his initiation into the mysteries of Sais. The Christ-child figure in Novalis' first chapter suggests that he too intended to link Sais with Christianity.

4. Gaier (pp. 95ff.) argues that each speaker tries to integrate the position of the others into his own. Accordingly he finds that the third speaker reverses himself in the second round.

5. Carlyle, II, 17; Maurice Maeterlinck, "Novalis," in *On Emerson and Other Essays*, transl. Montrose J. Moses (New York: Dodd, Mead, 1920), p. 113.

Chapter Five

1. Kuhn, p. 150.

2. Ibid., p. 39.

3. See Jürgen Habermas, *Strukturwandel der Öffentlichkeit* (Berlin: Luchterhand, 1962), p. 20ff.

4. For an account of the Romantic reactions to Spinoza, see Neubauer, "Intellektuelle, intellektuale und ästhetische Anschauung," *Deutsche Vierteljahrsschrift für Literaturwissenschaft und Geistesgeschichte*, 46 (1972), 294–319.

5. Novalis reported on July 20 from Teplitz that the Christian religion was "one of the central monads" of his meditations and that he had thereby discovered the "religion of the visible universe" (IV, 255).

6. Friedrich Schleiermacher, *Über die Religion. Reden an die Gebildeten unter ihren Verächtern* (Berlin: Unger, 1799), pp. 50–55.

7. Ibid., p. 259.

8. Ibid., p. 11.

9. Ibid., pp. 167–71.

10. Wilhelm Dilthey, *Aus Schleiermachers Leben* (Berlin: Reimer, 1860–63), III, 139.

11. Passage added to the second speech in the second edition of *Über die Religion*.

12. However, Novalis referred to the text merely as "Europa"; the subtitle of the 1826 edition, "Ein Fragment," seems unwarranted.

13. Dilthey, *Erlebnis*, p. 207. But Dilthey rightly criticized Novalis for abandoning the "real" foundations of historical progress toward unity in favor of a "dreamed divine peace" under the protection of religious conviction (ibid.). For similar criticism of *Christenheit*, see Korff, III, 330.

14. Jürgen Kreft sees in the simultaneous application of these philosophies of history the beginning of a dialectic concept of history: "Die Entstehung der dialektischen Geschichtsmetaphysik aus den Gestalten des utopischen Bewußtseins bei Novalis," *Deutsche Vierteljahrsschrift für Literaturwissenschaft und Geistesgeschichte*, 39 (1965), 213–45.

15. In the exhortation to wait patiently for the return of the sacred, Novalis echoes the central theme of Hölderlin's late hymns.

16. On the basis of this discrepancy between Novalis' interpretation of the past and his vision of the future, Wilfried Malsch has argued that *Christenheit* contains "first a narration about Europe and second an interpretation of this narration directed at Europe. All turns to the past, greeted or regretted in the reception of Novalis, belong exclusively to the narration which is interpreted by the speaker in terms of a historical typology. All possibilities pointing toward peace belong to the speaker's interpretation, who sees them prefigured in the narration and prophetically evokes them" (*'Europa' Poetische Rede des Novalis* [Stuttgart: Metzler, 1965], p. VI). Malsch's interpretation seems to impose upon the speech too severe a division.

Chapter Six

1. Carlyle, p. 44.

2. Arthur Rimbaud, letter to Paul Demeny of May 15, 1871, in *Oeuvres*, ed. Suzanne Bernard (Paris: Garnier, 1960), p. 346.

3. The three pentametric stanzas at the beginning of Hymn V represent the only exception to that rule, inasmuch as they contain a higher proportion of adjectives than some of the prose passages.

4. That is Max Kommerell's final judgment. Kommerell admires the *Hymnen* as a daring experiment which attempts to replace the lost order of life by a poetic and personal world view. Thus, in Kommerell's interpretation, the *Hymnen* do not end with an affirmation of the Christian community: Novalis becomes an early and major representative of aestheticist modern poetry ("Novalis: 'Hymnen an die Nacht,' " *Gedicht und Gedanke*, ed. Heinz Otto Burger [Halle: Niemeyer, 1942], pp. 212–36).

5. Quoted in the article on Oetinger in the *Allgemeine deutsche Biographie*, vol. 24, p. 539.

6. Karl Barth, *Protestant Theology in the Nineteenth Century. Its Background and History* (London: SCM Press, 1972), pp. 361 and 363. Barth believes that although Novalis represents Romanticism "with a certain unequivocality and finality" (p. 344), his writing shows ambiguity and unresolved tension between Christ and Maria, between the acceptance of an almighty and infinite God and the belief in infinitely expanding man.

7. Ibid., p. 377.

8. See Heinz Ritter, *Der unbekannte Novalis* (Göttingen: Sachse & Pohl, 1967), p. 151.

9. Dilthey, *Erlebnis*, p. 221.

10. *Nur* could also mean "merely" (instead of "the only"), and in this case the last line would amount to a depreciation, instead of a praise of power. I am grateful to Richard Samuel for calling this alternate reading to my attention.

11. See Walther Killy, *Über Georg Trakl*, 3rd ed. (Göttingen: Vandenhoeck & Ruprecht, 1967), esp. pp. 38–51.

12. Kant, *Kritik der Urteilskraft* (Berlin: Lagarde, 1790), p. 33f.

Chapter Seven

1. Johann Wolfgang Goethe, *Briefe*, ed. Karl Mandelkow (Hamburg: Wegner, 1964), II, 229f.

2. Schlegel, II, 182f. See also p. 57 above.

3. See Erich Heller's "Conversation on the Magic Mountain," reprinted in *Thomas Mann. A Collection of Critical Essays*, ed. Henry Hatfield (Englewood Cliffs, N.J.: Prentice-Hall, 1964), pp. 62–95.

4. Freedman remarks that in the lyrically conceived *Ofterdingen* "the hero's time-bound adventures are transformed into a sequence of image-scenes that mirror the nature of the protagonist's quest and represent it symbolically. The progression required by the narrative genre is converted into a lyrical progression produced by the elaboration of pictures and scenes" (p. 14). I should want to add that the images are mostly replaced by conversations.

5. These authorial intrusions are very clearly set apart from the rest of the novel, and their primary function is to reestablish the readers' critical distance from the narrative world.

6. Schlegel, *Lyceum* fragment no. 26, II, 149.

7. Cf. Freedman: the hero's function is self-reflexive, he is passive; "the figures of persons and things become part of an exquisitely woven pattern of tapestry, an artificial 'world' " (p. 9); "The hero becomes the receptacle of experience at the same time that he is its symbolizing agent" (p. 19); "narrator and protagonist combine to create a self in which experience is fashioned as imagery" (p. 31).

8. Elizabeth Sewell, *Signs and Cities* (Chapel Hill: University of North Carolina, 1968), p. 27.

9. See Richard Samuel, "Novalis: 'Heinrich von Ofterdingen,' " in *Der deutsche Roman*, ed. Benno von Wiese (Düsseldorf: Bagel, 1963), I, 285–98, for a reconstruction of Novalis' plan.

10. Reinhold Steig and Herman Grimm, *Achim von Arnim und die ihm nahe standen* (Stuttgart: Cotta, 1894–1913), I, 41. In the critical Novalis edition, this remark is erroneously attributed to Clemens Brentano (I, 190).

11. Ibid., I, 136.

12. Ibid., I, 51.

13. Carlyle, p. 45.

14. Maeterlinck, p. 110.

15. Dilthey, pp. 194, 233, and 325.

16. Hermann Hesse, *Gesammelte Werke* (Frankfurt/Main: Suhrkamp, 1970), XI, 108 and 113.

Chapter Eight

1. Gerhard Schulz sees no conflict between Novalis' profession and calling (*Novalis in Selbstzeugnissen und Bilddokumenten* [Hamburg: Rowohlt, 1969], p. 119); Hans Mayer, in turn, could not reconcile the poet of *Ofterdingen* with the state official (p. 25).

2. Jakob Baha, editor of Müller's *Die Elemente der Staatskunst* (Jena: Fischer, 1922), vastly overestimated Novalis' impact upon Müller. Baha (II, 264) believed that Novalis was the originator of the Romantic theory of state, and he traced passages in Müller to Novalis. But Müller probably did not know the unpublished parts of *Christenheit;* of the two passages in which he refers to Novalis' work (I, 234 and 258), one, on the self-milling mill, is taken out of context and misapplied.

3. Steig and Grimm, I, 66.

4. Quoted by Hans-Joachim Mähl, "Goethes Urteil über Novalis," *Jahrbuch des freien deutschen Hochstifts* (1967), p. 216.

5. Ibid., p. 254.

6. Johannes Falk, *Goethe aus näherm persönlichen Umgange dargestellt* (Leipzig: Brockhaus, 1832), pp. 98–100. The authenticity of Falk's report has been conclusively established by Mähl (p. 190ff.).

7. Franz Grillparzer, *Sämtliche Werke* (Munich: Hanser, 1964), III, 788f.

8. Heinrich Laube, *Geschichte der deutschen Literatur* (Stuttgart: Hallberger, 1839–40), III, 152f. However, the Hegelian Young Germans Arnold Ruge and Theodor Echtermeyer wrote one of the earliest appreciative essays on Novalis (rpt. in Schulz, ed. *Novalis* [Darmstadt: Wissenschaftliche Buchgesellschaft, 1970], pp. 1–19).

9. Heinrich Heine, *Sämtliche Schriften* (Munich: Hanser, 1971), III, 440f.

10. Joseph von Eichendorff, *Werke* III (Munich: Winkler, 1976), 27.

11. Ibid., III, 754.

12. Ibid., III, 761.

13. Ibid., III, 765ff.

14. Dilthey, p. 241.

15. Ibid., p. 211f and 324.

16. Ibid., p. 212ff.

17. Carlyle, p. 27.

18. Ibid., p. 51.

19. Ibid., p. 21.

20. Ibid., pp. 3 and 50.

21. Ibid., p. 29.

22. Ibid., p. 43f.

23. Ibid., p. 51.

24. Maeterlinck, p. 115.

25. See Rudolf Ernst Kuenzli, "The Reception of Novalis in England and America in the Nineteenth Century," dissertation, University of Wisconsin, 1972, esp. pp. 89–203. Kuenzli gives a detailed list of the nineteenth century English and American translations of Novalis. He also discusses references to him in the writings of De Quincey, George Eliot, Thomas Hardy, Henry Wadsworth Longfellow, and Walter Pater. Professor Gerhard Schulz (Melbourne) recently identified the epigraph of Joseph Conrad's *Lord Jim* ("It is certain my conviction gains infinitely, the moment another soul will believe in it.") as an adaptation of no. 153 in the "Brouillon": "Es ist qewiß, daß eine Meinung sehr viel gewinnt, sobald ich weiß, daß irgend jemand davon überzeugt ist—sie wahrhaft annimmt" (III, 269). I am grateful to Professor Schulz and Professor Siegbert Prawer for calling this to my attention and allowing its publication.

26. Ralph Waldo Emerson, *The Journals and Miscellaneous Notebooks*, ed. William H. Gilman et al. (Cambridge, Mass.: Harvard University Press, 1960), IV, 302. Emerson copied several of Novalis' remarks into his notebooks and made frequent references to him (e.g. IV, 300; V, 273; VIII, 69 and 485; and XII 155f.). Of particular interest are the Novalis passages that Emerson copied from Carlyle's essay into his "Encyclopedia" between 1824 and 1836 (VI, 104, 107, 128, 174, 202, 209, 219, and 222).

27. Emerson, "Goethe: or The Writer" (part of "Representative Men"), *Centenary Edition* (rpt. New York: AMS, 1968), IV, 280.

28. Emerson, *Journals*, XI, 259.

29. Poe used Novalis' note on the parallel between "ideal events" and reality (III, 669) as an epigraph for his tale *The Mystery of Marie Rogêt*. Kuenzli (pp. 184–93) discusses three additional references to Novalis in Poe's writing.

30. On Novalis and the French poets see Werner Vordtriede, *Novalis und die französischen Symbolisten* (Stuttgart: Kohlhammer, 1963); Lilian R. Furst, "Novalis' 'Hymnen an die Nacht' and Nerval's 'Aurelia'," *Comparative Literature*, 21 (1969), pp. 31–46; and Paul Gorceix, *Les affinités allemandes dans l'oeuvre de Maurice Maeterlinck* (Paris: Presses Universitaires de France, 1975), esp. pp. 66–113. Donald P. Haase ("Romantic Facts and Critical Myths: Novalis' Early Reception France," *The Comparatist*, 3 [1979], pp. 23–31) brings solid evidence for early acquaintance with Novalis in France.

31. Gottfried Benn recognized in Novalis one of the first modern poets (*Probleme der Lyrik*, in *Gesammelte Werke*, ed. Dieter Wellershoff [Wiesbaden: Limes 1960–68] IV, 1065). Hugo Friedrich's study, *Die Struktur der modernen Lyrik* (Hamburg: Rowohlt, 1956), themes and theoretical views that link Novalis with the French Symbolists.

32. André Gide, *Romans*, ed. Y. Davet and J. J. Thierry (Paris: Gallimard, 1958), p. 31. About Gide's reaction to Novalis, see also his letter to Paul Valéry of June 11, 1892, and his journal entries made in August 1893.

33. Maeterlinck, p. 60.

34. Ibid., pp. 88 and 83.

35. Georg Trakl, "An Novalis," *Dichtungen und Briefe*, ed. Walther Killy and Hans Szklenar (Salzburg: Müller, 1969), I, 325. The poem, of which there exists a significantly different version, was probably written in 1913.

36. Hesse, XII, 236.

37. For Novalis and Hesse see Theodore Ziolkowski, "Hermann Hesse and Novalis," dissertation, Yale University, 1957. Harry Haller, the "Steppenwolf," owns Novalis' works and is primarily interested in his notions on disease and the necessity of suffering (Hesse, VII, 193 and 196f.).

38. Thomas Mann, *Reden und Aufsätze* (Frankfurt/Main: Fischer, 1965), II, 32.

Selected Bibliography

1. Works by Novalis

Schriften. Ed. Paul Kluckhohn and Richard Samuel. 2nd. ed. 4 vols. Stuttgart: Kohlhammer, 1960–1975.
   vol. I: 3rd. ed. 1977
   (This historical-critical edition of Novalis' works, actually prepared by
   Richard Samuel, Hans-Joachim Mähl, and Gerhard Schulz, supersedes
   all previous editions. An index-volume is in preparation.)
Werke. Ed. Gerhard Schulz. Munich: Beck, 1969.
   (An excellent one-volume annotated edition of the poetic works, with
   generous selections from the theoretical writings. Based on the new
   historical-critical edition.)

2. English Translations of Novalis' Works (in chronological order)

Henry of Ofterdingen. Cambridge (Mass.): John Owen, 1842. 2nd ed. New
   York: H.H. Moore, 1853.
Christianity or Europe. Transl. John Dalton. London: Chapman, 1844.
Hymns and Thoughts on Religion. Transl. W. Hastie. Edinburgh: Clark,
   1888.
Novalis; his Life, Thoughts, and Works. Ed. M.J. Hope. Chicago: McClurg
   and London: Stott, 1891.
Hymns to the Night (sel.). Warner's Library of the World's Best Literature.
   Ed. Charles Dudley Warner. New York: Peale and Hill, 1897. XVIII,
   10727-32.
The Disciples at Sais and other Fragments. Transl. F.V.M.T. and U.C.B.
   Introd. Una Birch. London: Methuen, 1903.
Devotional Songs. Bilingual ed. Ed. Bernhard Pick. Chicago: Open Court,
   1910.
Hymns to the Night. Transl. Mabel Cotterell. Introd. August Closs. Lon-
   don: Phoenix, 1948.
The Novices of Sais. Transl. Ralph Manheim. Pref. Stephen Spender. 60
   drawings by Paul Klee. New York: C. Valentin, 1949.

176

Sacred Songs of Novalis. Transl. Eileen Hutchins, Aberdee: Selma, 1956.
Hymns to the Night and other Selected Writings. Transl. Charles E. Passage. New York: Liberal Arts, 1960.
Henry von Ofterdingen. Transl. Palmer Hilty. New York: Ungar, 1964.

SECONDARY SOURCES

1. English

Barth, Karl. "Novalis." *Protestant Theology in the Nineteenth Century. Its Background and History.* London: SCM Press, 1972. (Translation of the German original published in 1947.)
Carlyle, Thomas. "Novalis." *Critical and Miscellaneous Essays.* New York: Scribners, 1899. II, 1–55. (First published in 1829. A historically important essay which contains very little on the poetic works.)
Frye, Lawrence O. "Spatial Imagery in Novalis' 'Hymnen an die Nacht.' " *Deutsche Vierteljahrsschrift für Literaturwissenschaft und Geistesgeschichte,* 41 (1967), 568–91.
Furst, Lilian R. "Novalis' 'Hymnen an die Nacht' and Nerval's 'Aurélia.' " *Comparative Literaure,* 21 (1969), 31–46. (A sensitive comparison, based on themes and attitudes rather than "influence.")
Haywood, Bruce. *Novalis: The Veil of Imagery. A Study of the Poetic Works of Friedrich von Hardenberg* (1772-1801). The Hague: Mouton, 1959. (A perceptive and intelligent study in the "new criticism" tradition.)
Hiebel, Friedrich. *Novalis: German poet, European thinker, Christian mystic.* Chapel Hill: U.N.C. Press, 1954. (The only comprehensive treatment so far in English; attempts to line up Novalis with Rudolf Steiner's anthroposophy. The rev. and enlarged German ed. of 1972 utilizes the new critical edition and contains a useful bibliography.)
Maeterlinck, Maurice. "Novalis." *On Emerson and Other Essays.* Transl. Montrose J. Moses. New York: Dodd, Mead, 1920. 53–118. (The French original of 1895 has become part of Maeterlinck's *Le trésor des humbles.*)
Neubauer, John. *Bifocal Vision. Novalis' Philosophy of Nature and Disease.* Chapel Hill: U.N.C. Press, 1971. (Mainly on Novalis' studies in medicine, physiology, and biology.)
Rehder, Helmut. "Novalis and Shakespeare." *PMLA,* 63 (1948), 604–24.
Schaber, Steven. "Novalis' Theory of the Work of Art as Hieroglyph." *Germanic Review,* 48 (1973), 35–43. "Novalis' 'Monolog' and Hofmannsthal's 'Ein Brief'. " *GQ,* 47 (1974), 204–14.
Stopp, Elisabeth. " 'Übergang vom Roman zur Mythologie'. Formal Aspects of the Opening Chapter of Hardenberg's Heinrich von Ofterdingen, Part II." *Deutsche Vierteljahrsschrift für Literaturwissenschaft und Geistesgeschichte,* 48 (1974), 318–41.

von Molnár, Géza. *Novalis' 'Fichte Studies.' The Foundations of his Aesthetics.* The Hague: Mouton, 1970. "The Composition of Novalis' 'Die Lehrlinge zu Sais': A Reevaluation." *PMLA,* 85 (1970), 1002–14.

2. German

Dick, Manfred. *Die Entwicklung des Gedankens der Poesie in den Fragmenten des Novalis.* Bonn: Bouvier, 1967.

Dilthey, Wilhelm. "Novalis." *Das Erlebnis und die Dichtung.* Göttingen: Vandenhoeck, 1965. 187–241. (Originally published in 1865.)

Faber, Richard. *Novalis: Die Phantasie an die Macht.* Stuttgart: Metzler, 1970.

Gaier, Ulrich. *Krumme Regel. Novalis' 'Konstruktionslehre des schaffenden Geistes' und ihre Tradition.* Tübingen: Niemeyer, 1970.

Haering, Theodor. *Novalis als Philosoph.* Stuttgart: Kohlhammer, 1954.

Hamburger, Käte. "Novalis und die Mathematik." *Philosophie der Dichter.* Stuttgart: Kohlhammer, 1966. 11–82. (Original published in 1929.)

Heftrich, Eckhard. *Novalis. Vom Logos der Poesie.* Frankfurt/M.: Klostermann, 1969.

Heukenkamp, Ursula. "Die Wiederentdeckung des 'Wegs nach innen.' Über die Ursachen der Novalis-Renaissance in der gegenwärtigen bürgerlichen Literaturwissenschaft." *Weimarer Beiträge,* 19 (1973), 105–28. (An orthodox Marxist attack on Western interest in Novalis.)

Kapitza, Peter. *Die frühromantische Theorie der Mischung. Über den Zusammenhang von romantischer Dichtungstheorie und zeitgenössischer Chemie.* Munich: Hueber, 1968.

Kesting, Marianne. "Aspekte des absoluten Buches bei Novalis und Mallarmé." *Euphorion,* 68 (1974), 420-36.

Kommerell, Max. "Novalis: 'Hymnen an die Nacht.' " *Gedicht und Gedanke.* Ed. Heinz Otto Burger (Halle: Niemeyer, 1942), 212–36.

Kreft, Jürgen. "Die Entstehung der dialektischen Geschichtsmetaphysik aus den Gestalten des utopischen Bewußtseins bei Novalis." *Deutsche Vierteljahrsschrift für Literaturwissenschaft und Geistesgeschichte,* 39 (1965), pp. 213–45.

Küpper, Peter. *Die Zeit als Erlebnis des Novalis.* Köln: Böhlau 1959.

Kuhn, Hugo. "Poetische Synthesis oder Ein kritischer Versuch über romantische Philosophie und Poesie aus Novalis' Fragmenten." *Zeitschrift für philosophische Forschung,* 5 (1950-51), 161–78 and 358–84. (An excellent comprehensive and critical essay based on a textual analysis of a longer note in the "Brouillon.")

Kuhn, Hans Wolfgang. *Der Apokalyptiker und die Politik. Studien zur Staatsphilosophie des Novalis.* Freiburg: Rombach, 1961.

Link, Hannelore. *Abstraktion und Poesie im Werk des Novalis.* Stuttgart: Kohlhammer, 1971.

Lukács, Georg. "Novalis." *Die Seele und die Formen.* Berlin: Fleischel, 1911. 93–117.

Mähl, Hans-Joachim. *Die Idee des goldenen Zeitalters im Werk des Novalis. Studien zur Wesensbestimmung der frühromantischen Utopie und zu ihren ideengeschichtlichen Voraussetzungen.* Heidelberg: Winter, 1965. (A seminal study of the concept of "golden age" in Novalis; half of the book is taken up by an erudite historical tracing of the concept.) "Novalis und Plotin. Untersuchungen zu einer neuen Edition und Interpretation des 'Allgemeinen Brouillon.'" *Jahrbuch des freien deutschen Hochstifts.* 1963. 139–250. (An excellent case study of Novalis' "Brouillon" and a demonstration of the brilliant work that went into the new historical-critical edition.) Ed. *Dichter über ihre Dichtungen: Novalis.* Munich: Heimeran, 1976. (A complete collection of Novalis' remarks about his own works.) "Friedrich von Hardenberg (Novalis)." *Deutsche Dichter der Romantik.* Ed. Benno von Wiese. Berlin: Erich Schmidt, 1971. 190–224.

Mahr, Johannes. *Übergang zum Endlichen. Der Weg des Dichters in Novalis' 'Heinrich von Ofterdingen.'* Munich, Fink, 1970. (A close study of the text.)

Paschek, Carl. *Der Einfluββ Jacob Böhmes auf das Werk Friedrich von Hardenbergs (Novalis).* Unpubl.diss. Bonn 1967.

Ritter, Heinz. *Der unbekannte Novalis.* Göttingen: Sachse & Pohl, 1967. (Mostly studies of manuscript versions of Novalis' poetic works.)

Samuel, Richard. *Die poetische Staats- und Geschichtsauffassung Friedrich von Hardenbergs (Novalis). Studien zur romantischen Geschichtsphilosophie.* Frankfurt: Diesterweg, 1925. (Still the most important work on Novalis' concept of history and politics.) "Die Form von Friedrich von Hardenbergs Abhandlung 'Die Christenheit oder Europa.'" *Stoffe Formen Strukturen. Festschrift H.H. Borcherdt.* Ed. A. Fuchs and H. Motekat. Munich: Hueber, 1962), 284–302. (A structural analysis of *Christendom.*) "Novalis. Heinrich von Ofterdingen." *Der deutsche Roman. Struktur und Geschichte.* Ed. Benno v. Wiese (Düsseldorf: Bagel, 1963), I, 252–300.

Schanze, Helmut. *Romantik und Aufklärung. Untersuchungen zu Friedrich Schlegel und Novalis.* Nürnberg: Hans Carl, 1966.

Schulz, Gerhard. "Die Poetik des Romans bei Novalis." *Jahrbuch des freien deutschen Hochstifts.* 1964. 120–57. (Best account of Novalis' theory of fiction.) *Novalis in Selbstzeugnissen und Bilddokumenten.* Hamburg: Rowohlt, 1969. (A judicious account of Novalis' life and work through biographical documents.) *Novalis. Beiträge zu Werk und Persönlichkeit Friedrich von Hardenbergs.* Darmstadt: Wissenschaftliche Buchgesellschaft, 1970. (A collection of articles; reprints of Kommerell, Hugo Kuhn, Lukács, Mähl, Walzel, and Schulz' own important account of Novalis' professional career.)

Striedter, Jurij. "Die Komposition der 'Lehrlinge zu Sais.'" *Der Deutschunterricht,* 7 (1955), 5–23.

Träger, Claus. "Novalis und die ideologische Restauration, Über den ro mantischen Ursprung einer methodischen Apolgetik." *Sinn und Form,* 13 (1961), 618–60.

Vordtriede, Werner. *Novalis und die französischen Symbolisten.* Stuttgart: Kohlhammer, 1963. (A tracing of themes, images, and notions of symbolism.)

Walzel, Oskar. "Die Formkunst von Hardenbergs 'Heinrich von Ofterdingen.'" *Germanisch-romanische Monatsschrift,* 7 (1915–19), 403–44 and 465–79. (A good study of Novalis' novelistic technique in relation to *Wilhelm Meister.*)

Wetzels, Walter D. "Klingsohrs Märchen als Science Fiction." *Monatshefte,* 65 (1973), 167–75.

Ziegler, Klaus. "Die Religiosität des Novalis im Spiegel der 'Hymnen an die Nacht," *Zeitschrift für deutsche Philologie,* 70 (1948/49), 396–418 and 71(1951/52), 256–77.

Index